G000144573

Walks in I
with a
Pushchair

Hilary Bradnam

Illustrations by Beryl Bradnam

First Edition: June 2002

Published by Hilary Books
ISBN: 0-9533315-2-0

ACKNOWLEDGEMENTS:

I would like to thank all those who have helped in the
production of this book, especially the Field Studies Council
at Rhyd-y-Creuau and the Forestry Commission
for their resources and advice,
Laura Booth, Beryl and Colin Bradnam, Pauline Pritchard,
and Lorna Shipp for accompanying me
on walks and for their advice.
Finally to my partner, Martin Smith, for his constant
support at every stage of the production of this book,
and to Joshua for sitting in the pushchair.

Printed by Gwasg Carreg Gwalch
12 Iard yr Orsaf, Llanrwst, Dyffryn Conwy LL26 0EH
(01492) 642031 (01492) 641502

Enquiries regarding sales:

Hilary Books,
Betws-y-Coed

Tel: 01690 710741

E-mail: hilarybooks@aol.com

To Joshua

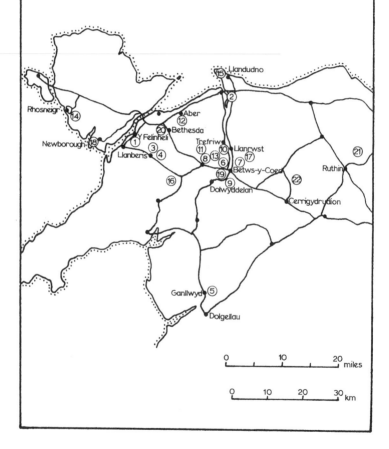

LOCATION OF WALKS

- • Village / Town
- ④ Walk number

Llandudno ⑮
②
Rhosneigr ⑭
Aber
⑫ Bethesda
Newborough ⑱ ⑳ Y Felinheli
① Trefriw
Llanberis ③ ④ ⑪ ⑩ Llanrwst
⑧ ⑬ ⑰
⑥ ⑦ ㉑
⑯ ⑲ Betws-y-Coed Ruthin
⑨ ㉒
Dolwyddelan Cerrigydrudion

Ganllwyd ⑤
Dolgellau

0   10   20 miles

0   10   20   30 km

4

Walks in North Wales with a Pushchair

CONTENTS

Introduction

This book has been written after I found myself limited to tarmac road and promenades, once my son became too heavy for the backpack. Determined not to be separated from the mountains and countryside until I could dispense with the pushchair, I explored many known, and also previously unknown, paths and tracks, often without success. Gradually I realized I had discovered something that many other parents would be looking for.

Every route has been walked several times with my son in his pushchair in a variety of conditions to ascertain its suitability, and all have been undertaken with a standard light-weight buggy, **not** an all-terrain pushchair.

The walks include forest, farmland, mountains and coasts, using a variety of tracks, paths and old railway lines. The area covered ranges from Anglesey in the north to Coed-y-Brenin in the south, from Caernarfon in the west to Offa's Dyke in the east.

I have classified the walks loosely into easy, moderate and intrepid, based on length, total ascent, number of stiles and kissing gates, and the nature of the surface, but do read the details at the beginning of each walk before starting, to check it is what you are expecting. I have tried to be as accurate and to provide as much detail as possible.

All routes follow public rights of way or recognised courtesy paths such as Forestry Commission tracks. However, please do not use this book alone as justification for access. Also note that where reference has been made to field gates as possible alternatives to kissing gates or stiles, they are not necessarily on public rights of way and could be padlocked without warning.

The book is designed to be used without O.S. maps, but if you want to buy the relevant maps they are:

1:50 000 Landranger Series	Anglesey	Sheet 114
	Snowdonia	Sheet 115
	Denbigh, Colwyn Bay	Sheet 116
	Dolgellau	Sheet 124

All the areas are also covered by the Outdoor Leisure and Explorer Series at 1:25 000.

Background information is provided in italics separately from the directions to help you find your way. Distances for driving are given in miles only, but for walking they are given in both miles and kilometres. Shorter distances are given in metres.

This is a Welsh speaking area, so where Welsh words are in common usage, these names have been used. The following translations may be useful:

Afon / river   Llyn / lake   Moel / ridge   Pont / bridge

The walks have been chosen with families in mind. **Where it is advisable to go ahead of children e.g. on the approach to a waterfall or an unavoidable road crossing, you will find an !.** In the countryside there are many natural hazards, so please do not assume that the sign ! marks every steep slope, deep pool etc.

Remember the country code. Some warnings: avoid areas where forestry work is taking place, no vehicles are allowed on Forestry Commission tracks without permission, old mines and quarries can be dangerous. Dogs are unpopular in many farming areas, so please keep them under control, particularly in the lambing season.

While every endeavour has been made to be accurate, changes occur in the countryside. I would be grateful for information about blocked footpaths or confusing changes which have occurred, and would welcome comments and criticisms.

Be prepared for some mud, some effort but lots of rewards, and I hope that you and your children enjoy yourselves.

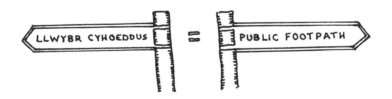

KEY TO THE MAPS

——	Road
====	Track
– – –	Path
—+—+—	Railway line
→	Route
～～	River or stream
▰	Lake
⌢⌢	Coastline
▪ ▢	Building, Ruin
♁	Church or chapel
✳	Place of interest
▲	Triangulation pillar
⌒	Quarry
⽊	Coniferous forest
♤	Broadleafed woodland
☀	Viewpoint
P	Parking
T	Telephone box
km	Kilometres

1 Lôn Las and the Menai Straits

This is an easy, flat walk along an old railway line (now also a cycle route), starting in Y Felinheli, with views across the Menai Straits for much of its length. It finishes in Caernarfon with plenty of attractions, including the castle, the harbour and numerous cafes. It is not a circular walk but the return journey can be made by bus. The number 5/5A can be picked up in the town centre or above the Safeway's car park. Buses are approximately two per hour.

Distance:	3³/₄ miles / 6 km
Total ascent:	0m
Surface:	Tarmac or fine gravel
No. of stiles:	0
No. of kissing gates:	0
Need to pull or carry:	No
For map, see page 10	

HOW TO GET THERE: From the A487 east of Caernarfon, take the B4547 through Y Felinheli (Port Dinorwic on older maps). At the west end of the town, turn down Rowen opposite the church, signposted to Traeth/Beach (the beach is not an attractive one). The old railway line crosses the road 50m down. There is limited parking here, or at the bottom by the boatyard.

DIRECTIONS: Turn along the Lôn Las cycle path at the noticeboard, with the Menai Straits on your right. It starts as a tarmac path past the wooden barrier.

> *The route follows the old Bangor to Caernarfon railway. It was opened in 1851 and was one of the earliest passenger railways in the area. It survived the Beeching cuts but was closed in January 1972. Much of the way is wooded as a result of the trees which have grown up in the intervening years. In the first cutting, the banks have become a haven for wild flowers, including primroses, wood anemones, wild garlic, pussy willow and buddleia.*

After passing under a bridge, the path opens up.

> *The sculptures are by a local sculptor, Valerie Coffin Price and were placed here in 1998. There is also a picnic bench here, although the traffic on the main road is fairly close.*

LON LAS AND THE MENAI STRAITS

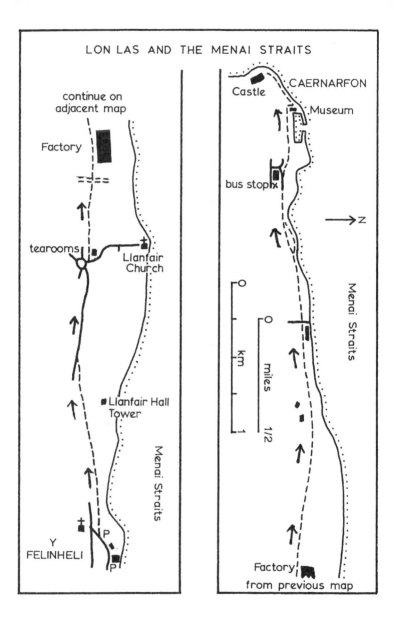

Continue along the path, passing on your right, the tower of Llanfair Hall. As the path joins the road, the tarmac stops and it becomes a smooth stony path on the grass verge. There follows a 650m stretch on the pavement alongside the road, ending at a roundabout.

The Country Manor tearooms are open 7 days a week (except Thursdays out of season). They are very child-friendly with toys provided both inside and outside.

Cross the minor road on your right, signed to Plas Menai and Cemetery. It is worth a detour to the church and viewpoint 450m down the road.

Detour: Walk down the road for 300m. Continue straight past Plas Menai, the National Watersports Centre, to the church. A path to the left leads down to a small stony beach.

LLANFAIR CHURCH

The church of Llanfair dates back to the 13th century and despite much restoration over the years, the walls and bell-cote are from this period. It was the parish church of Y Felinheli until larger congregations required a bigger church and it was replaced by the new St. Mary's in 1865. It has a large number of stained glass windows, although one window has been re-used in the barn at Plas Llanfair. Sadly, the church is kept locked, but the key is available from the Vicarage by the new church. The views along the Menai Straits are to Caernarfon to the west and towards Britannia Bridge to the east.

11

To continue: At the far side of the roundabout, pick up the signs for the cycle route to the right of the crash barrier. After 50m, pass under or round the wooden barrier on a fine gravel path as it finally leaves the main road. Continue for another 500m and cross another minor road via two wooden barriers. Here you pass the Ferodo Factory which manufactures car components. You may notice a slight smell as you pass.

The next stretch to the outskirts of Caernarfon is more rural, closing with the Menai Straits as it crosses two small bridges.

Here you pass two large mansions, with recently landscaped grounds, indicative of Caernarfon's former glory in the 19th century. Now these two buildings comprise a 5 star hotel.

After passing a row of houses on your right hand side, including the old station, you reach another minor road. A 40m detour down to the Menai Straits brings you to a good stone throwing beach.

Continue through the barrier ahead along the path. Pass through the fence and keep to the central level path, ignoring any paths to left or right. Follow the coastline round, and at the next wooden barrier go straight ahead. Bear left past the jetty on your right and join the road end, keeping the Straits on your right.

There is a proposal to develop the waste land adjacent to the Straits. The plans are for a Celtic Centre, including retailing and tourist attractions, to be built towards the end of 2002. Any changes to this section of the walk will be signposted as it is also a recognised cycle route.

Walk down the pavement ahead towards the masts; then follow the path around the dock, passing between the dock and the car park. Cross the footbridge over the slip, and at the end of the dock turn right past the small Maritime Museum to the sea wall. Turn left along the walkway around the outside of the town walls to reach the castle, harbour and town centre.

Return by the same route or catch the bus (details at the start of this walk.)

2 RSPB Conwy

The Nature Reserve lies on the estuary of the Afon Conwy opposite the town of Conwy, and provides a flat, easy walk. It is surprisingly peaceful considering its proximity to the A55. It is worth visiting even if you are not interested in birds as the views are good and there are posts containing children's activities throughout the walk. It is open 10-5 every day, with a charge of £2.50 for non-members. Children and RSPB members are free, no dogs. There are plans to create a Harry Potter Owl Trail for children. N.B. Cuddfan means Hide.

Distance:	**1¹/₂ miles / 2.5 km**
Total ascent:	**0m**
Surface:	**Stony paths**
No. of stiles:	**0**
No. of kissing gates:	**0**
Need to pull or carry:	**No**
For map, see page 14	

HOW TO GET THERE: Leave the A55 at the A546 signed to Llandudno Junction and Deganwy. At the roundabout follow the signs down the road as it sweeps left into the main car park.

DIRECTIONS: From the car park, the entrance is through the building via reception and the shop. Turn right and pass post 1 to follow a boardwalk through reeds, passing post 2. Bear right and pass post 3, then turn right at the next junction to the first hide, containing posts 4 and 5.

The reserve and the lagoons were created in 1995 as part of a deal with the construction company of the new Conwy Tunnel which had been completed a few years earlier. Spoil from the tunnel was allowed to be dumped on the site provided that a nature reserve was created.

On leaving the hide, retrace your steps back to the path junction and turn right.

Ahead, on the skyline lies the obelisk in the grounds of Bodysgallen Hall. This is not a Victorian folly, but was constructed controversially in the 1990's.

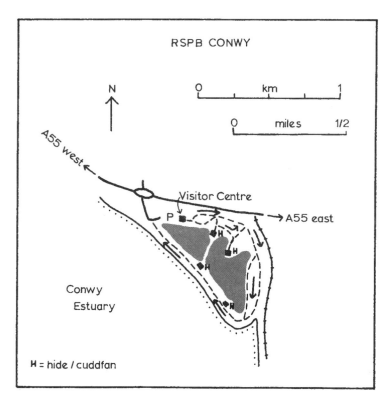

Cross the bridge over the lagoon at post 6, and pass through the gate to the lapwing conservation area. Turn right at the next junction to the second hide.

This hide has a similar view to the first one but contains post 7 and also coloured identification pictures of all the birds you are likely to see; essential for the non-experts.

From the second hide, retrace your steps to the path junction, and continue straight on, then turn right at the next junction onto a wider track. This track swings south heading up the Conwy Valley. At the signpost 'Cuddfan Foel Fras Hide 650m', you have a choice.

Either: If you are interested in birds, flowers and butterflies, turn right to follow a winding grassy path between reeds and meadow. Continue following the path to signs to 'Cuddfan Foel Fras 190m.'

Or: If you are more interested in the estuary and a good view of the trains, go straight on. After 600m the paths rejoin at the fence. With the estuary on your left, go through the gate and continue towards the hide.

CONWY ESTUARY

Here is the best panoramic view. Looking up the Conwy Valley, the Carneddau Mountains lie to your right. Further down is Conwy, with Brunel's railway bridge almost hiding the castle. The twin hills of the Vardre can also be seen where there are the remains of a Norman castle. The castle was destroyed by Edward I when he built Conwy Castle in case it posed a threat to him.

Cuddfan Foel Fras Hide is on your right. It is divided into two, to provide views over both the lagoons and the estuary. Continue along the main path and follow the estuary, passing Cuddfan Benarth Hide on your right. At the gate the path leads back into the car park.

3 Llanberis: Slate and Lakes

This is the first of two walks in the Llanberis area, both on the theme of slate. The second, **'Dinorwic: Slate and Views'** can be found on page 21. It is a fairly easy walk which takes you round the edge of Llyn Padarn (with plenty of ducks to feed) to the Padarn Country Park. From there you rise up through the lower part of the slate quarry and return via the Welsh Slate Museum. The museum is free and there is the option of returning to the car park on the ferry in the summer or going for a ride on the Llanberis Lake Railway. The walk includes a flight of 64 steps down.

Distance:	**3 miles / 5 km**
Total ascent:	**30m**
Surface:	**Grassy paths, muddy if wet, tarmac road and stony paths**
No. of stiles:	**0**
No. of kissing gates:	**1, just negotiable**
Need to pull or carry:	**Up 4 steps**

HOW TO GET THERE: Take the A4086 to Llanberis. On the Llanberis by-pass, park in the 'Village Car Park' which is a narrow strip between the main road and the lake. Parking is free at the time of going to print.

DIRECTIONS: Cross the grassy bank to the lake and turn right through the gap in the fence to follow the path adjacent to the water. There are usually plenty of water birds wanting to be fed along this stretch.

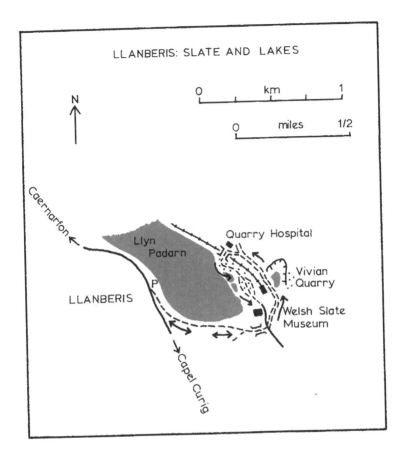

LLANBERIS: SLATE AND LAKES

Caernarfon

Llyn Padarn

LLANBERIS

P

Quarry Hospital

Vivian Quarry

Welsh Slate Museum

Capel Curig

Across the lake you can see the old Quarry Hospital, the highest point of the walk, nestling in the trees. Where the hillside has not been quarried, the slopes are covered in oak trees. This woodland, Coed Dinorwig, is a fragment of an ancient woodland which covered all the lower slopes of Snowdonia after the Ice Age. However, in most areas, the trees have been cleared to make way for agriculture. Coed Dinorwig has survived because the rough terrain makes it unsuitable for farming.

After the children's playground, cross the stream by a footbridge (to the left of the trees and the playground). At the car park, bear left to cross a second footbridge, and enter the Padarn Country Park.

From here follow the wide grassy path as it continues near the lake shores. Pass close to the redundant kissing gate, and then go through the next kissing gate which is just negotiable. Cross a small wooden footbridge over a ditch and continue on the grassy path, winding between rushes in the general direction of the cream house on the hillside. Pass a line of trees and cross a third footbridge to leave the stone building on your left. Turn left over the bridge across the Afon Nant Peris (the gate is heavy).

Go straight across the road and head up the hill past Glen-y-Bala on your right. Continue past the 'No Entry' signs and pass under the bridge which supports an incline. Just around the bend after the bridge, it is possible to turn left between walls to view the incline. Return to the road and carry on for 50m to Vivian Quarry.

The quarry on your right was first excavated in the early 1800's and finally closed in 1964. Once the pumps were switched off, it filled with water to a depth of 20m. Now it is used for diving and for rock climbing. Gradually plants are growing on the bare rock as the slate weathers very slowly.

At the end of the slate retaining wall on your right, pass under the second incline.

This inclined tramway was built in 1866 and after falling into disrepair has been restored to working order. The heavy slate-laden trucks descend the incline by gravity, pulling up the lighter empty trucks to the top thus avoiding the need for power. All the slate was then transported to Y Felinheli, on the coast, along what is now the Llanberis Lake Railway.

Enter the Quarry Hospital grounds and fork left to pass in front of the buildings.

The hospital was built in the 1860's for the employees of the quarry. It is now a museum and, although some of the instruments look more suitable for torture, it had the first x-ray machine in Wales. Beyond the hospital lies the mortuary, unfortunately used all too frequently.

Turn down the slate steps between the railings. There follows a flight of 64 wooden steps to cross high above the Llanberis Lake Railway and then up 4 awkward steps to reach a flattened area.

You are standing on the top of an old slate spoil heap which used to rise up to the level of the top of the wooden steps. A bridge at that level used to support a tramway which carried the slate from the Vivian Quarry. The slate was tipped into the lake, and the base of this heap is 30m below water level.

Take the path which sweeps left, passing a useful labelled sketch of the view ahead.

Llyn Padarn is the 6th deepest lake in Wales. It contains a rare fish called an Arctic Char which is believed to have survived in the waters since the Ice Age over 10,000 years ago. On the pointed hill below Moel Eilio lies Dinas Ty Du, an iron-age hill fort.

As the Welsh Slate Museum comes into view, a network of paths criss-cross the smaller spoil heaps and skirt the lagoons below. Take any one of them to reach the main car park.

GILFACH DDU

The museum is housed in what were the workshops for the whole Dinorwic quarry and it provides an insight to the lives of the 15,000 people who worked in the quarry in its heyday. It contains the second largest water wheel in Britain and there are regular demonstrations of slate splitting. It is open all year, but not Saturdays from November to Easter.

Once in the car park, it is worth making a detour to visit the Vivian Quarry under the arch you have previously walked over. From the car park you can return either by ferry (June to September) or, to walk, head down the road with the museum on your right. Immediately past the museum building, turn right over the bridge and retrace your steps along the lake shore to the car park.

4 Dinorwic: Quarry and Views

Slate quarrying has been such an important feature of North Wales that a walk through the quarries seems essential. This is a fairly easy walk, starting in the small village of Dinorwic on the slopes above Llanberis. It crosses both reclaimed and original slate areas, culminating in a spectacular view over Llanberis and the Snowdon range. To walk through the other half of the slate quarries and to visit the slate museum, turn to Llanberis: Slate and Lakes on page 16.

Distance:	**2¹/₂ miles / 4 km**
Total ascent:	**100m (or 50m if you return by the road)**
Surface:	**Tarmac, grassy paths, slate paths**
No. of stiles:	**0**
No. of kissing gates:	**1, just negotiable**
Need to pull or carry:	**No**
For map, see page 22	

HOW TO GET THERE: From Llanberis, take the A4086 towards Caernarfon. At the end of Llyn Padarn, turn right on the B4547, signed to Bangor and Deiniolen. After 200m, take the first right, and then right again signed to Fachwen. Follow the winding single track road to the top. Turn right, and then, after 250m, turn right again at cross roads into Bro Elidir to park.

DIRECTIONS: Walk down the hill signposted as a 'No Through Road' with a playground on your right. At the road end, just past the old slate covered chapel, continue straight ahead on the track downhill. Pass to the left of the cottages, and through the wooden gate to the left of the field gate. Once in the field, follow the grassy path to the right.

This area was reclaimed between 1984 and 1986 as, prior to that, the cliff to your left beyond the road was a deep quarry. The huge whole was filled with slate waste and at the same time the area was landscaped and planted with grass. The stream in its concrete channel frequently has fascinating flow patterns down the chute.

Cross the bridge over the leat and continue along the main path which rises up as it skirts the fenced area on your left.

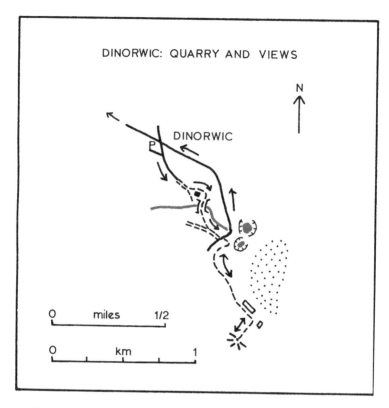

DINORWIC: QUARRY AND VIEWS

DINORWIC

N

miles   1/2

km   1

*The spoil heaps rising ahead are a classic feature of this area.
The waste could be as much as 20 times the amount of usable
slate, hence the huge slate heaps across this whole area.*

Join the stony track and continue uphill, taking the right fork near the
top. At the road, turn left and then immediately right into the bus turning
area. Go through the kissing gate to the right of the large gate; it is just
negotiable. The first 100m are a bit rough, but once round the bend it
is easier going. Follow the stony, walled path as far as the large ruin
and pass to the right of the two buildings. At the second building, turn
right to the end. **! There are steep drops but they are fenced.** A
spectacular view opens up ahead and below.

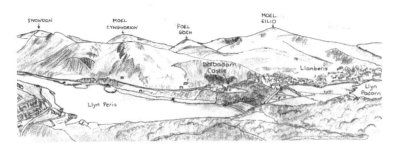

You are now standing on a long finger of slate waste overlooking the main quarry. To your left is Llyn Peris which is the lower reservoir for the Dinorwic Pumped Storage Power Station. Power is generated by allowing the water to come from the upper reservoir at Marchllyn Mawr down to Llyn Peris. During times when there is excess electricity being generated by other power stations, the water is pumped back up to the top. The lake levels therefore fluctuate. All the power station buildings are hidden underground in the old quarry to your left where three million tonnes of rock were removed. The cavern is twice the length of a football pitch and is higher than a 16-storey building.

Retrace your steps to your car, or alternatively, on reaching the bus turning area, turn right along the road back to the crossroads, then left into Bro Elidir.

5 Goldmines and Waterfalls Walk

This walk lies within Coed-y-Brenin, a large forest between Blaenau Ffestiniog and Dolgellau. It follows the valley of the Afon Mawddach to its confluence with the Afon Gain where the two waterfalls make a spectacular sight. It passes through both coniferous plantations and broad leafed woodland and predominantly is on easy stone tracks. For added interest there are the remains of the old goldmines. At the time of going to print, the bridge at Rhaeadr Mawddach cannot be crossed due to flood damage. It is due to be repaired but while the repairs are being carried out, a temporary foot bridge will be put in place on the downstream side. In summer it is a leafy walk, whereas in winter the river gorge is clearly visible.

Distance:	**4 miles / 6 km**
Total ascent:	**80m**
Surface:	**Stony tracks**
No. of stiles:	**0**
No. of kissing gates:	**0**
Need to pull or carry:	**No**

HOW TO GET THERE: Take the A470 from Blaenau Ffestiniog towards Dolgellau. After 16 miles, immediately beyond the 40mph sign at Ganllwyd, turn sharp left on an unsigned minor road. Bear right after the bridge, and then follow the single track road through trees to Tyddyn Gwladys car park on the right.

DIRECTIONS: Turn right out of the car park and continue along the road to the end. At the sign 'Ferndale, private road', take the lower track, using the small footpath on the right if the gate is padlocked. At Ferndale, bear left past the barrier to continue along the track. After 550m, at the top of a rise, ruined buildings are visible on the left.

These buildings were not part of the goldmine but are the remains of a blasting powder works, built not just for the Gwynmynydd goldmine further up, but also for all the goldmines in the area. The ruin with the stream next to it held the water wheel which powered machinery to grind the blasting powder. Technology progressed shortly after the construction of these works and they soon became redundant. As you pass the second building you get your first views of Rhaeadr Mawddach just above the confluence of the two rivers.

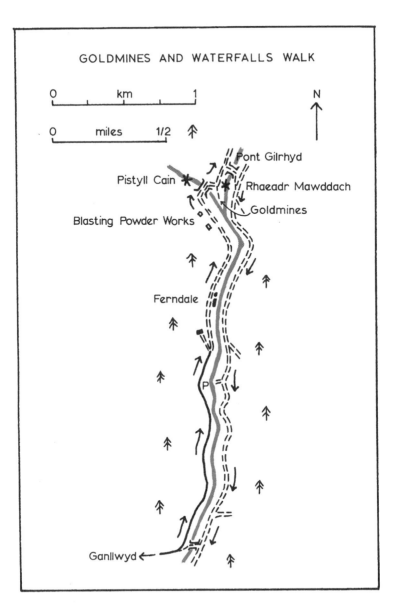

GOLDMINES AND WATERFALLS WALK

Pont Gilrhyd

Pistyll Cain

Rhaeadr Mawddach

Goldmines

Blasting Powder Works

Ferndale

P

Ganllwyd

The track sweeps right over a bridge across the Afon Gain with views upstream of Pistyll Y Cain. After 35m, turn right down the track to the viewpoint of Rhaeadr Mawddach. This is a 50m detour and involves pulling the pushchair back, but is well worth the effort. It is possible to walk to the end of the rocky outcrop for the best views of the waterfall and the confluence. **! There are unprotected drops.**

The scattered ruins in this area are the remains of Gwynfynydd Mine, a successful goldmine from 1840 to the beginning of the 20th century. It was temporarily opened in the 1980's but has been closed for about 13 years. The mine itself was located higher up, but this area was used for water power. Unfortunately, the tours referred to on the notice board are no longer available.

Return to the track, turn right and continue to the second bridge passing, on your right, the channels which carried the water from the river to power the mine.

PONT GILRHYD

Pont Gilrhyd crosses the Afon Mawddach. It is reputed to be 300-400 years old but was damaged in the floods in July 2001. Despite the upper stone work being destroyed, the underlying arch remains intact, indicating the strength of its construction. (This is the bridge which is uncrossable due to flood damage at the time of going to print).

Turn right over Pont Gilrhyd, and then after the steep rise, turn right again along the forestry track.

As the waterfall comes into view again, it is easier to see (in winter) how extensive the mine buildings used to be.

At the track junction, just after Ferndale on the opposite bank, take the right hand fork. Ignore the steep rough track leading down to the river opposite the car park, but keep to the main track, ignoring the track joining from the left at a gate. Turn right over a wooden footbridge and bear left uphill. It is a bit rough but is only 50m to the road. Turn right back to the car park.

6 Two Rivers Walk

Starting and finishing in the centre of Betws-y-Coed, this is a short, flat walk on the floor of the Conwy Valley. It follows the banks of the Afon Llugwy and returns along the Afon Conwy. Although short, the path can be muddy after rain and tends to become rather overgrown in summer, resulting in some awkward sections.

Distance:	**1¹/₂ mile / 2.5 km**
Total ascent:	**0m**
Surface:	**Grassy paths, some muddy sections**
No. of stiles:	**0**
No. of kissing gates:	**3, 1 is just negotiable**
Need to pull or carry:	**Over 2 kissing gates, and pull on muddy or overgrown areas**

HOW TO GET THERE: Take the A5 to Betws-y-Coed and park in one of the many car parks.

DIRECTIONS: Opposite the Royal Oak Hotel, take the road through the small car park and follow the tarmac to the Royal Oak Stables, which now houses the Information Centre. Turn left through the white gate signed 'Private Road', with a footpath sign. After 150m the track narrows and gradually becomes a footpath as the surface becomes rougher. The woodland path passes under the railway bridge and the next 100m can be hard going. The path is narrow with tree roots; it can be muddy after heavy rain but is always passable except when flooded. At the gateway to the golf course, keep to the river bank.

(This next section along the river behind the fence can be avoided by turning right immediately before the kissing gate and keeping to the edge of the mown grass). The kissing gate is just wide enough for a pushchair, before going down a few steps to the bench. **! The rivers are fast flowing in spate and the Afon Llugwy has a sewage treatment works just upstream.**

Here is the confluence of the Afon Llugwy on your left and the Afon Conwy on your right. After periods of heavy rain, the colour of the water from the two rivers is distinctly different. The Afon Llugwy, with its head waters in the mountains, is usually clear, while the Afon Conwy which rises on the moorland is a peaty brown. During floods the river level may cover the bench. Above the two rivers is the Aberllyn Gorge down which tumbles a stream, another tributary of the Conwy.

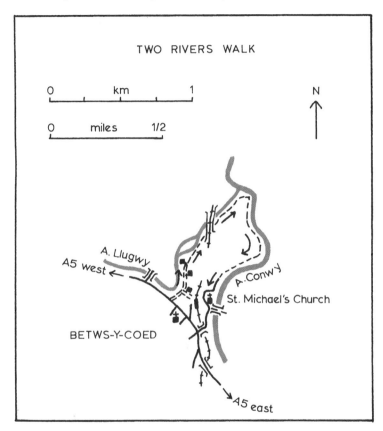

TWO RIVERS WALK

BETWS-Y-COED

A. Llugwy

A5 west ←

A. Conwy

St. Michael's Church

A5 east

N

Turn right at the bench to follow the Afon Conwy upstream. The next 50m are narrow and tends to get overgrown by stinging nettles. At the kissing gate which is rather narrow, the walk returns to the golf course, where you need to keep to the river bank. **! Beware of golf balls.** Bear left down the steps and continue round the golf course. Where the signs indicate the path should pass between the fence and the river, it is badly eroded by flooding and there are 100m where it is necessary to pull or carry, depending on conditions.

Conditions improve at the kissing gate, which is narrow, and there follows another woodland walk to the road.

St. Michael's Church

St. Michael's Church was built in the 14th century and was used as the parish church until tourism necessitated a larger one to be built in Victorian times. At one time a gallery existed at the back of the church and this was used for the village school. There is a stone effigy of Gruffydd ap Dafydd Goch who used to live at Fedw Deg. The font is 13th century indicating there may have been an earlier church on the site. When locked, the key is available from the Railway Museum or the Information Centre.

Join the road to skirt the church and graveyard on your left, while on your right is the Railway Museum with its miniature railway. Cross the railway line by a bridge to return to the main road.

7 A Walk to Picnic Point

Garthmyn, or Picnic Point is one of the most spectacular view points in Snowdonia and can be reached with little effort. It is an easy, fairly flat walk across the slopes to the east of the Conwy Valley above Betws-y-Coed. The path can be muddy in winter or overgrown in summer. The last 50m to the view point are not suitable for a pushchair.

Distance:	**1 mile / 1.5 km**
Total ascent:	**40m**
Surface:	**Mud and grassy paths**
No. of stiles:	**1**
No. of kissing gates:	**1 but avoidable**
Need to pull or carry:	**Pull up 24 steps but they can usually be avoided**
	Pull on some muddy or overgrown areas

For map, see page 32

HOW TO GET THERE: From Betws-y-Coed, take the A470 towards Llanrwst. After less than $^1/_2$ mile, turn right up the steep, single track road, signposted to Capel Garmon. Immediately past the row of cottages on your left, park adjacent to the telephone box.

DIRECTIONS: The official path starts 10m below the telephone box at a footpath sign. It passes through an awkward kissing gate and, keeping the wall to your left, rises up a flight of 24 stone steps. At the top, it joins the drive. However, at the time of going to print, there appears to be no objection to using the drive which starts immediately above the telephone box.

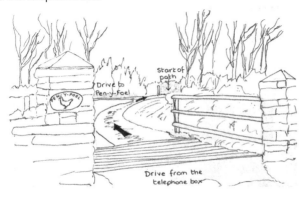

31

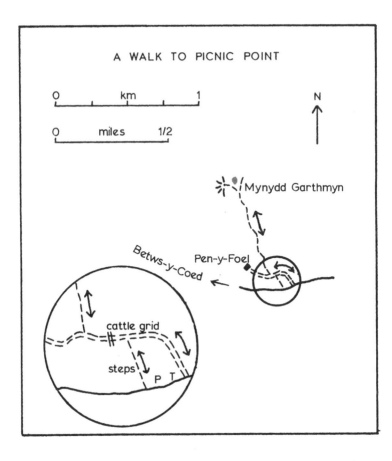

A WALK TO PICNIC POINT

Follow the drive through the gateway over a cattle grid (the pushchair wheels can get stuck between the rails).

After 30m, turn right along a grassy path which passes between bracken and gorse. For most of the way it is possible to push but there are some muddy sections and in summer it can be overgrown. After 350m you reach a stile.

Once across the stile, pass to the right of a low rocky outcrop immediately in front of you, and then bear left along the wide grassy path. Cross the grassy dip and then bear right up a short steep rise between bracken. 30m after the top, the path bears left, then right, but generally as it winds, keep the mountains to your left.

As you approach a rocky knoll on your left, the path divides. Follow the arrow on the wooden signpost uphill to the left. As you rise, a pool appears to your right below. It may be necessary to leave the pushchair here as the last 50m to the view point are rocky. **! There are steep unprotected drops.**

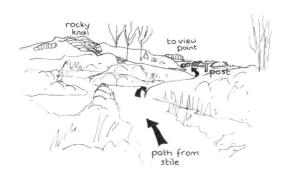

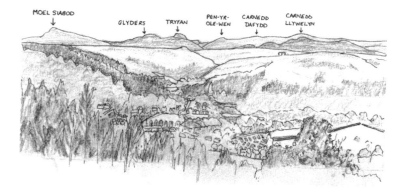

As long ago as Victorian times this place was marked as Picnic Point on maps and it has been a popular spot ever since. Northwards there are views along the Conwy Valley and beyond. Below lies the village of Betws-y-Coed in its stunning location nestling among the forested slopes. Westwards lie the mountains of Snowdonia; most are visible except for Snowdon itself.

Return to your car by the same route.

8 Swallow Falls

The waterfall is one of the most famous in the country and due to the frequent rain in the nearby mountains, it is spectacular at most times of the year. The walk is an easy, gentle walk on forest tracks until the immediate vicinity of the falls where the ground is rougher and tends to be muddy. As an alternative to this walk there is pavement all the way up the A5 from Betws-y-Coed to view the falls from the official platform for which there is a small charge.

Distance:	**1$^1/_2$ miles / 2 km**
Total ascent:	**40m**
Surface:	**Stony track except near the falls where it is a rough, muddy path**
No. of stiles:	**0**
No. of kissing gates:	**0**
Need to pull or carry:	**Pull along 20m of track, pull or carry in the waterfall area**

For map, see page 36

HOW TO GET THERE: Take the A5 from Betws-y-Coed towards Capel Curig for 2$^1/_2$ miles, past the Swallow Falls Hotel, to the sharp bend over the river. Immediately across the bridge, take the steep, single track road adjacent to the Ugly House. After the Towers Outdoor Education Centre, turn right on the forest track and park at the side.

DIRECTIONS: Walk down the track through the beech trees. At the fork, take the right track downhill. Continue gently downhill until the track parallels the river about 30m to your right. Where a wide path forks left uphill, your track narrows to a path and continues straight ahead (marked by a yellow topped post). There follows a 20m stony stretch where it is necessary to pull the pushchair. At the junction in paths, turn sharp right down the steep stony path towards the falls. It is impossible to take the pushchair beyond the stream, but you are within 30m of the viewing area at the top of the falls. **! There is a fence but there are steep drops.**

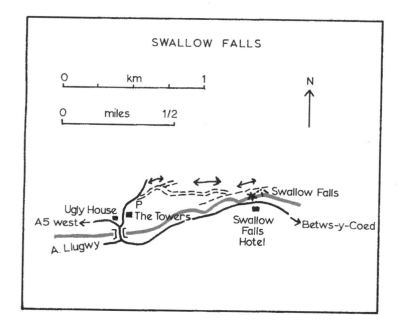

SWALLOW FALLS

The original name of the falls was Rhaeadr Ewynnol, meaning Foaming Falls but this has been mistaken in the past for Rhaeadr-y-Wennol, meaning Swallow Falls, and the incorrect name is now used. It is claimed that Sir John Wynne, a local landowner, has been condemned to purgatory in the falls since 1627 and his moaning can still be heard.

Return to the pushchair and retrace your steps to the path junction.

For the intrepid: It is possible to reach the lower viewing area. Continue straight on keeping the river on your right. The narrow path is just negotiable by pulling the pushchair and the steep drops are protected by a fence. At the wooden fencing turn right down the steep zigzag path to the bench. It is worth the effort; even my two-year-old was impressed by the view!

The falls cascade down in two sections although, in times of flood, the two join together and the viewing platform on the far side can be submerged.

SWALLOW FALLS

From either viewpoint, return by the same route.

9 Lledr Valley Walk

The outward leg of this peaceful valley walk from Pont-y-Pant, meanders along the valley floor alongside the Afon Lledr and the railway line, while the return leg rises higher up the valley side passing through the forest with fine views of the mountains. Although the terrain is varied, it is fairly easy going for most of the walk but after very heavy rain the valley floor can be under water. The village of Dolwyddelan lies at the half way point with a shop and pubs a few hundred metres off the route.

Distance:	**4¹/₂ miles / 7 km**
Total ascent:	**90m**
Surface:	**Stony tracks, tarmac, some grassy or mud paths**
No. of stiles:	**1, but usually avoidable**
No. of kissing gates:	**0**
Need to pull or carry:	**No**

HOW TO GET THERE: Turn off the A470 between Betws-y-Coed and Dolwyddelan, signed to Pont-y-Pant Station. At the T-junction turn right and continue for a further 100m. Parking is limited, but the road is widest **on** the bridge over the railway line, where the road bears left.

DIRECTIONS: Continue along the road, past the station. After 650m, pass though a gate where it becomes a dirt track but still easy going. At the top of a rise, the surface becomes grassy as it passes through the right hand edge of a field before dropping on a more rutted path parallel to the railway line. After a second gate, bear right under the railway line. This section is currently very rutted following a storm in July 2001. Immediately under the bridge bear left along a clear grassy track across the valley pastures. In places there are the remains of a very old paved path. After passing two cottages and a gate, the surface improves again and it becomes a semi-tarmac track.

Just after crossing the stream, on your right in the trees, are the remains of an oxbow lake. The curved area of water represents the former course of the Afon Lledr. The old clapper bridge was constructed to carry a tramway for the slate trucks from the quarry on the hillside above the current railway line. It is still possible to see the foundations of the old inclined tramway above you on your left.

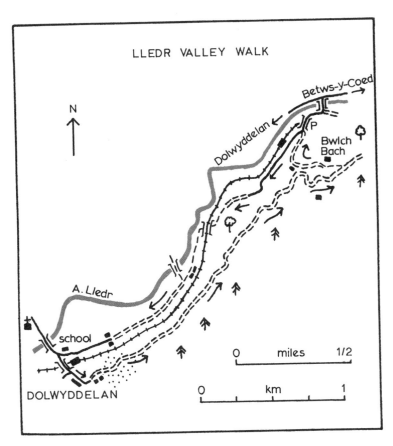

LLEDR VALLEY WALK

Betws-y-Coed

Dolwyddelan

Bwlch
Bach

P

A. Lledr

school

DOLWYDDELAN

0   miles   1/2

0   km   1

Ignore the signed path to your right over the bridge across the river. The next gate leads you into a farmyard. Pass straight through between the farm buildings and continue on the tarmac road past the school and the railway station to the T-junction.

A detour to the right brings you into the centre of Dolwyddelan with its two shops, two pubs and a historic church well worth visiting. The key is available from 1, Pentrefelin (walk to the main road, turn right, house on left beyond Elen's Castle Hotel) or from 4, Glan Aber (cross railway bridge, turn right, house on left).

To continue on the walk, turn sharp left over the railway bridge, then immediately left again at the post box in the wall to follow the main tarmaced road uphill (signposted 'no through road). Pass the cottages and, at the end of the terrace on your right, turn left along the track. Pass more houses on your right, then cross the ladder stile to the left of the gate which is usually unpadlocked.

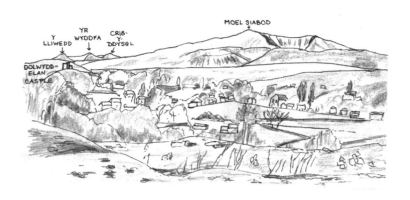

The slate tips are from the Ty'n-y-bryn quarry which was worked in the 19th century. From here there is a good view point over Dolwyddelan. It is possible to see the square keep of the 12th century castle below, with Moel Siabod towering above. On a clear day, to the left of Moel Siabod, you can also see the slopes of the Snowdon Massif with the peaks of Y Lliwedd, Yr Wyddfa and Crib-y-Ddysgl.

40

Continue on the gated forestry road for the next 2 miles (3 km) ignoring the track which turns left before the slate spoil heaps. You pass through patches of forest but in between there are splendid view points in areas of pasture and open woodland of beech and birch. 300m after the third gate, the track swings in a very tight bend into the hillside, with a renovated farmhouse clearly visible in a field to the right of the road on the edge of the forest. Continue along the forest track to enter a coniferous plantation at a fourth gate. 175m further along the road turn sharp left down a rough stony path. At the large house of Bwlch Bach on your right, the surface improves and it widens to a track as it winds downhill to the road at the start of your walk.

10 Afon Conwy to Trefriw

This is a flat walk along the banks of the Afon Conwy, starting in Llanrwst, and returning across the floodplain. It is easy going apart from the nine stiles. Despite being low-lying the path is rarely muddy as it follows the flood control embankments and returns on a tarmac path. It is a quiet walk which incorporates the village of Trefriw with its woollen mill, child-friendly pub and children's playground.

Distance:	**2³/₄ miles / 4.5 km**
Total ascent:	**0m**
Surface:	**Grassy path and tarmac path**
No. of stiles:	**9**
No. of kissing gates:	**1, but usually avoidable**
Need to pull or carry:	**Only lifting over small stiles**

HOW TO GET THERE: From Llanrwst Square, take the A470 towards Llandudno. After 450m, fork left along Station Yard, (signed to the station), and park at the end on the right hand side adjacent to the station wall.

DIRECTIONS: Leave the Yard by the entrance you have driven in, and immediately turn right along a tarmac road, past Llanrwst workshops and the Vet's surgery.

Cross Gower's Bridge over the Afon Conwy. Immediately over the bridge, at a footpath sign, turn right over a small stile where the route now follows the embankment for the next 1¹/₂ miles (2.5km). Cross the 2nd stile at a left hand bend.

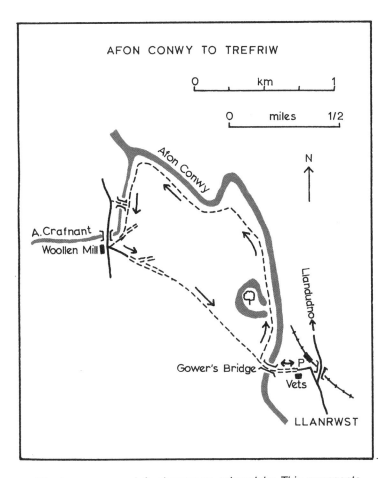

AFON CONWY TO TREFRIW

The trees, on your left, obscure an oxbow lake. This represents the course along which the Afon Conwy originally flowed, but with frequent floods the river gradually eroded a new, straighter course to your right. The lake sometimes dries in summer as it is now separated from the main river by the man-made embankment on which you are walking.

Continue across a further 2 stiles, after which there is a fence to your right and gorse bushes to your left. After the 5th stile, as the embankment swings left again, a couple of gorse bushes have become overgrown making the path awkward to negotiate in places. .

To your right, across the river, a green hut is visible at Tan Lan which marks the tidal limit of the river. Despite being 10 miles (16km) from the sea the land is only 8m above sea level.

The embankment now rejoins the river bank. Cross 2 more stiles after which the path sweeps left, away from the main river, to follow the banks of the Afon Crafnant.

Just as you leave the Afon Conwy you cross a wide ditch with sluice gates under the path. These are designed to remain closed as floodwater comes up the river, but to allow floodwaters to return to the sea. During the winter months flooding is a common phenomenon, hence the embankments.

Follow the Afon Crafnant upstream to cross the 8th stile. Ignore the footbridge over the river but continue to the kissing gate. This is too narrow for pushchairs but the field gate is rarely padlocked. Continue up the farm track for 50m, and then leave the track at a footpath sign to cross the 9th (and final) stile. Follow the narrow path to a seating area in Trefriw.

Opposite lies the woollen mill which has operated here since 1859 using power from the waterfall on the Afon Crafnant. Guided tours are available. In Victorian times, paddle steamers and rowing boats came up the river bringing as many as 1000 people per day to take the waters at Trefriw Spa just outside the village. During World War 2, silting of the river prevented this from continuing. Now, Trefriw offers several cafes and shops, 2 pubs, and public toilets in the car park.

To continue the walk, from the seating area, turn left down the tarmac road signed to the playground. Pass the caravan site and the car park. The road narrows to a path and, from the children's playground, is virtually traffic free. The path is signed as a 'no through road' but leads back to Gower's Bridge from where you started the walk.

11 A Walk Around Llyn Crafnant

This gentle walk above the Conwy Valley takes you around a beautiful lake with some spectacular crags surrounding it. Most of the walk is on forest track or minor tarmac road (minimal traffic). However, there is one stretch down a steep path where it necessary to carry the pushchair (45m). There are many places adjacent to the lake for picnics, and a café is open in the summer months.

Distance:	3 miles / 5 km
Total ascent:	80m
Surface:	Track, tarmac and short path
No. of stiles:	1
No. of kissing gates:	1 necessary to lift
Need to pull or carry:	250m pull, 45m carry
For map, see page 46	

HOW TO GET THERE: Take the B5106 to Trefriw, and then turn up the very steep hill opposite the Fairy Falls Pub signposted to Llanrhychwyn, Llyn Geirionydd, Llyn Crafnant and Llyn Cowlyd. Follow this road for approximately 2 miles to the signed forest car park on your right.

DIRECTIONS: Leave the car park by the main entrance, turn right, and follow the road for 350m to the lake. **! This is a narrow winding road.** At the lake, turn right over the stream and through the kissing gate (necessary to lift the pushchair).

LLYN CRAFNANT

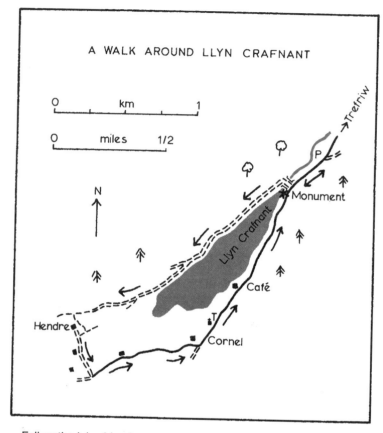

A WALK AROUND LLYN CRAFNANT

Follow the lakeside along a stony track. In many places it is possible to walk down to the lake shore. At the start of the forest, take the left hand fork in tracks (slightly downhill) and continue along the lakeside. After 250m, at a stream, the track is rough for 50m where it is necessary to pull the pushchair. Just after a dip, the track rises steeply and the surface deteriorates, necessitating a pull to the top.

As the track starts to flatten and narrows to a path, two posts mark the path down on the left.

This is a carry and it may be easier to fold the pushchair away, but it is only 45m. The first stretch is rocky and includes a ladder stile, but, as the path enters coniferous trees, it flattens and the surface has been improved with stones. (Any of the minor paths leading off rejoin lower down). Keep going to the bottom, ignoring the gate to Hendre on your

right, and continue to a metal gate. Pass through the gate and turn right over a wooden footbridge.

Hendre and Hafod are common names for farms. Hendre (winter dwelling) and Hafod (summer dwelling) are reminders of the time when farmers moved with their animals to use the higher pastures in summer. In the past there were more cattle (needing supervision and milking) than sheep on the hills.

Turn left along the track, through the gate and straight on to the end. Here turn left again through the gate and follow the tarmac road along the lakeside, passing Cornel (now a scout centre), and a former Congregationalist chapel. About halfway along, there is a café on your left.

Llyn Crafnant has been a reservoir since 1896 and the monument at the far end of the lake commemorates this. The lake is now used for fishing as well as a water supply and is stocked with trout, bred in the tanks just opposite the café.

Follow the road down to the car park.

12 Aber Falls

This walk, near the North Wales coast, follows the Afon Aber, a beautiful rocky river which flows from the spectacular Aber Falls, where the walk ends. It is on a clear and popular path, mostly with a gravel surface, but it is rough in places. It passes through the nature reserve of Coedydd Aber and has the optional return on a more intrepid path through the forest which involves crossing a scree slope.

Distance:	**2³/₄ miles / 4.5 km**
Total ascent:	**120m, (160m with the alternative return)**
Surface:	**Stony path, rough in places, (muddy path on alternative return)**
No. of stiles:	**0 (2 on alternative return)**
No. of kissing gates:	**All wide and easily negotiable**
Need to pull or carry:	**No (250m pull up scree on alternative return)**

HOW TO GET THERE: From the A55 take the turning signposted to Abergwyngregyn. Follow the signs to Rhaeadr Aber Falls. Park 1 mile up the single track road on the right hand side, just before the sharp left turn over the river. If this area is full, continue over the bridge and immediately turn right to the Forestry Commission car park which has toilets.

DIRECTIONS: 1. From roadside car park (rocky footpath): At the top end of the parking area, go through the wide kissing gate and take

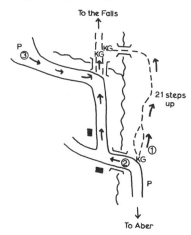

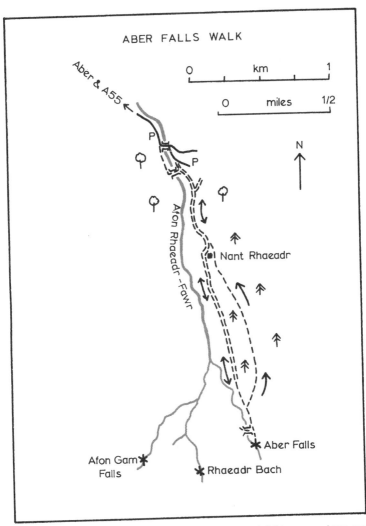

ABER FALLS WALK

the right fork in paths. The path continues up 21 fairly easy steps over a rocky area with a fenced drop and then sweeps left over a footbridge across the river. Continue up to the gates and lift the pushchair over the narrow kissing gate. At the main track turn right.

2. From the roadside car park (avoiding rocky footpath): Take the road over the river and immediately turn right following signs to the

49

car park. After 150m, as the road sweeps left uphill, continue straight on along the track with the sign 'Please keep this entrance clear' passing through the wide kissing gate.

3. From the Forestry Commission car park: Walk back down the road and after 100m turn left along the track with the sign 'Please keep this entrance clear', passing through a wide kissing gate.

Continuation for all three starts: The wide gravel track rises gently until, at a picnic bench on your left, you have your first glimpse of the waterfall and mountains ahead.

The mountains visible are on the northern end of the Carneddau, a range extending 6 miles (10 km) south to the Ogwen Valley. Much of the ridge is over 1000m, but Llwytmor to your left and Drosgl to your right are 690m and 758m high respectively.

Ignore the path forking left which is the route of the intrepid return and continue up the main track as it sweeps right around the old cottage.

This cottage, Nant Rhaeadr, is in a well-chosen spot with views down to the Menai Straits and Anglesey. It was a 'tyddyn', a typical smallholding, but it also provided teas for Victorian visitors to the falls. Alas, no more, as it now houses a small exhibition about the geology, geography and wildlife of the area. There are also old photos illustrating the clog-making industry

50

which used to thrive using the coppiced alder trees, and charcoal making has been re-established.

CHARCOAL BURNERS

Return to the track and carry on up. As the falls come into sight there is a split in the path. The right hand gravel path is easier, but they rejoin at the top of a rocky bluff. Pass through the wide kissing gate where the path dips before its final rise to the waterfall viewpoint.

Aber Falls is one of three waterfalls which tumble over the amphitheatre created by glacial erosion. In the winter it freezes and in summer may be reduced to a trickle, but the plunge pool at its base is always deep and cold. At 33m high, it is famous for its rippling patterns in the flow of water.

Return by the same route or follow the intrepid return.

Intrepid return: Retrace your steps to the kissing gate but don't go through. Turn right to climb the ladder stile signed 'return path through the plantation'. Take the path diagonally left up the hillside. It is narrow, rocky and bumpy and necessary to pull the pushchair, but, apart from the odd rock, there is nothing worse than the initial stretch. Continue to the ladder stile to enter the larch and spruce plantation.

There is a fine view back to Aber Falls and the whole amphitheatre. The second waterfall, Rhaeadr Bach, is also visible while the falls on the Afon Gam are hidden in the third valley.

51

ABER FALLS

The main path slowly descends through the woods and can be muddy. At a sign post on the left it is possible to make a 140m detour to a 'historical feature'. However it is steep and not feasible to take a pushchair.

The 'historical feature' is a small stone enclosure. The stone walls are the remains of a 13th century 'hafod', a summer dwelling. The stones have been reworked to create firstly an 18th century shepherd's hut and later 19th century sheep folds.

Continue along the main path which remains mostly mud with some tree roots although there are a few stony sections.

As you approach a field on your left, the trees change from spruce to larch. There is an immediately noticeable increase in light and undergrowth due to a change from evergreen to deciduous trees. In spring there are many woodland flowers including bluebells.

The path flattens out and it becomes a pleasant woodland walk. At the ladder stile it is usually possible to go through the gate and there is sufficient space for small children to crawl under it. The path gradually drops down to the outward route where you turn right to return to the car park.

13 Lakes and Forest Walk

The two lakes of Llyn Sarnau and Llyn Parc lie in the Gwydir Forest, north of Betws-y-Coed, and the walk undulates across the Nant Plateau between them. Apart from forestry there is plenty of farmland providing views of the nearby mountains. It is a fairly gentle walk on forest tracks, apart from one steep descent, and the return climb which is on a single track tarmac road.

Distance:	**4 miles / 7 km**
Total ascent:	**160m**
Surface:	**Stony tracks**
No. of stiles:	**0**
No. of kissing gates:	**0**
Need to pull or carry:	**No**

HOW TO GET THERE: From Betws-y-Coed, take the B5106 towards Trefriw. After 3 miles, just before the T-junction, turn left up the single track road, signed to Llyn Geirionydd. After $1^3/_4$ miles as the road flattens out, turn left into the small forestry car park, adjacent to the lake.

DIRECTIONS: From the car park entrance, turn right along the forest track with the fence to your left and the picnic bench to your right. Take the right fork and continue along the track over the causeway between the two lakes (which dry up in summer).

Across the lake to your right is the summit of Moel Siabod with an old miner's cottage on the side of the lake. To your left are some of the waste rocks from the lead mines in the area, these being the first of many signs of the old lead mines you will pass on the walk. In the lake itself during the summer, it is common to see cotton grass growing.

LLYN SARNAU & MOEL SIABOD

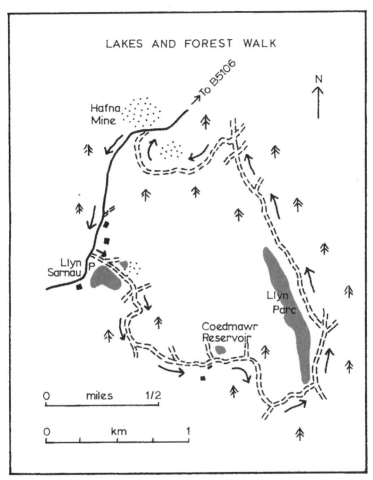

LAKES AND FOREST WALK

Hafna Mine

To B5106

N

Llyn Sarnau

P

Llyn Parc

Coedmawr Reservoir

0   miles   1/2

0   km   1

Continue uphill to the cross roads and go straight on past the yellow and black barrier. Once over the brow of the hill, the track winds down to a large rocky outcrop on your left. Here, turn left uphill. Ignore the track which joins from the left at the top of the hill.

At this point, in good weather, it is possible to see the summit of Snowdon behind you.

Immediately past the barns with corrugated iron roofs, bear right at the junction keeping the wall of Coedmawr Reservoir on your left.

Continue straight on at the next junction, and then at the T-junction, in a felled area, turn left. At the bottom of the hill lies Llyn Parc.

This lake has been used as a reservoir in the past for water power for the mines in the Aberllyn Gorge below. The deep greenish colour is due to the high mineral content of the water. It is not suitable for swimming as the water is cold and deep in the middle. In 1964, high lake levels forced water down into the Conwy Valley below, flooding across farmland and infilling the railway cutting with lead polluted sediment. The fields have never recovered completely and since, then, lake levels have been lowered.

At the T-junction at the lake end, bear left to keep the lake on your left. At the next junction of tracks, take the left track. At the fork in the tracks, after passing a long cliff face above you to the left, take the narrower left track downhill. **! The next section through broadleafed trees is steep downhill and is bumpy.**
Ignore the paths joining from left and right, and also ignore the grassy track crossing diagonally just before the telegraph poles. Continue for a further 35m to the next diagonal track. Turn left, as you have a glimpse of the Conwy Valley below.

There is much evidence of mine workings around here with fenced off shafts and old buildings. The Parc Mine was the most recent to close, with the last miners leaving in 1960. As you walk along the track, there is evidence, on your right, of the old Nant Uchaf tailing lagoon. Here, the tailings (waste rock from the crushing mill) were discharged from a peripheral pipe system. The coarse particles settled first and were heaped to form a bank around the edge of the pond.

Continue to the barrier to join the road.

Opposite lies Hafna Mine. The remains of the chimney are still there although the spoil heaps were reclaimed in the 1990's. Prior to that it was possible to find small pieces of discarded lead and zinc ore on the heaps.

Turn left uphill on the single track tarmac road to return to the car park. **! Watch out for traffic.**

14 A Walk Around Llyn Maelog

Llyn Maelog is a peaceful lake in the west of Anglesey, around which is a short and fairly flat path. Most of the walk is easy going and there are only a few rough stretches. However it does have nine stiles and six kissing gates. Five of the kissing gates are usually negotiable or can be bypassed using nearby gates, but eight of the stiles have to be crossed. The wildlife is varied and plentiful: it is common to see many birds including swans, greylag geese, cormorants, oystercatchers, moorhens and coots. There are also horses, donkeys and rabbits so every thing is there for the nature-lover! On weekdays there is the added attraction or intrusion (depending on your viewpoint) of jets taking off and landing at nearby RAF Valley. There is a nearby sandy beach.

Distance:	**2 miles / 3 km**
Total ascent:	**10m**
Surface:	**Tarmac, grassy paths, some rocky sections**
No. of stiles:	**9 although 1 is usually avoidable**
No. of kissing gates:	**6 although 2 are negotiable and 3 usually avoidable**
Need to pull or carry:	**Over stiles and kissing gates and several short rocky sections**

For map, see page 58

HOW TO GET THERE: Take the A55 dual carriageway across Anglesey. After 13 miles turn left on the A4080 signed to Rhosneigr. At Llanfaelog, by the post office, turn right and continue into Rhosneigr. At the clock tower follow the main road round to the left. After the de-restricted signs, park anywhere along the left hand side of the road.

DIRECTIONS: Continue to walk along the road in the same direction. **! The traffic travels fast** but there is a wide verge. Turn left along the track at the footpath sign adjacent to Plas-y-Ward B&B. Follow the track past three houses on the right hand side. As the third drive sweeps right at a white post, continue straight ahead on the grassy track. The kissing gate is narrow but the field gate is not padlocked. Once past the gate, bear left towards the lake and follow the lake edge. A gap in an old field boundary can just be negotiated by pulling the pushchair. At the next boundary either climb the stile or lift the pushchair over the stones which are all that remain of an old wall.

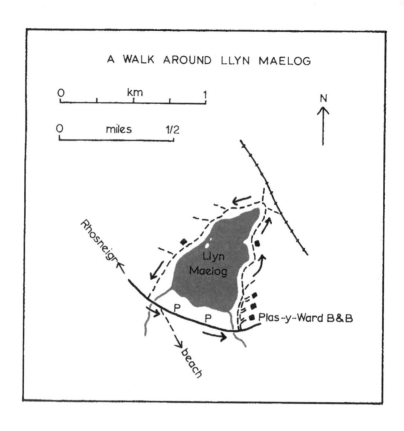

A WALK AROUND LLYN MAELOG

Llyn Maelog

Rhosneigr

Plas-y-Ward B&B

beach

hidden
kissing gate

ladder stile

kissing gate with
gap to left

gap in
wall

Continue to cross a stream and then a kissing gate. It is narrow, but at the time of going to print there is a wide gap to the left of the fence. Keep between the lake and the gorse to the next ladder stile. Cross the stile which is followed, 20m later, by a kissing gate, too narrow to pass through. However, there is a gate to the right which appears to be left open. From the kissing gate bear right and take the grassy path between gorse bushes with the house on your right. At the top of the rise, rejoin the lake shore and follow it to the head of the lake.

The entire length of the lake can be seen from here. In summer months it is used by wind surfers whereas in the winter there are more birds. The railway line is the main London to Holyhead line which connects with the ferry to Ireland.

It is necessary to carry the pushchair the last 10m to the bridge and also over the two stiles either side of the stream. From here, carry straight on until you are past the gorse bushes on your left, then turn left along the wide, grassy hollow. As you approach the lake shore again, bear right up a grassy path which heads towards the stile on the skyline. It is necessary to pull the pushchair near the top over a 10m rocky section. At the top by a yellow post, continue across the grass to the stile previously seen on the skyline. It is usually possible to by-pass this stile by going through the gateway 20m to your right and rejoining the path. This also avoids the rough ground.

CORMORANTS ON LLYN MAELOG

Head towards the next yellow post by the lake edge (to the left of the caravans) just beyond a shallow stream with irises growing in it. Pull the pushchair over a rough rocky section through a thicket which culminates in an awkward rock to lift the pushchair over. There follows a clear path to the next ladder stile which is painted yellow.

The wall marks the boundary of the Ty Hen Nature Reserve which won the David Bellamy Gold Conservation Award in 1999/2000.

Stay beside the reeds on your left through the next field heading towards the roof top visible over the hill, finally rising up to a yellow post. Wind through the gorse bushes and down a flight of 8 concrete steps to pass to the left of the house. The next kissing gate is narrow and unavoidable, leading onto a 5m rocky patch where the pushchair needs to be pulled.

The rocks on your left are smoothed and rounded, with deep grooves running across them. These were formed when a thick ice sheet covered the whole of Anglesey over 10,000 years ago, and boulders frozen into the base of the ice scraped away the bedrock like sandpaper.

Cross three more fields and three more stiles, then follow the path between the fence and the reeds. Bypass the next kissing gate and continue along the path between fence and reeds to a footbridge. At last there is a friendly kissing gate to go through, leading out onto the road. Turn left along the pavement to your car.

15 Great Orme's Head

The Great Orme is a large limestone headland, adjacent to Llandudno, most of which is designated as a Country Park. It has sea on three sides of it, and the views as you walk around the top include the Conwy valley, the mountains of Snowdonia, the Menai Straits and Anglesey. On a clear day the Isle of Man and the Blackpool Tower are also visible. It has a surprisingly wild feel about it, despite its close proximity to Llandudno. Most of the walk is easy, but it involves a steep descent at the beginning and a steep ascent at the end.

Distance:	**3 miles / 4.5 km**
Total ascent:	**90m (60m at end)**
Surface:	**Stony tracks and grassy paths**
No. of stiles:	**0**
No. of kissing gates:	**0**
Need to pull or carry:	**No**
For map, see page 62	

HOW TO GET THERE: Take the A470 to the centre of Llandudno. Follow Mostyn Street to its upper end. At the T-junction, turn right and then immediately left up Tŷ Gwyn Road, signed to the Copper Mines. The road does a hairpin left as it rises steeply. Cross the tramway and follow the main road for 1 mile to the summit car park for which there is a small charge. There is a shop, café and an information centre on the summit. N.B. Most of the walk is following the Great Orme Nature Trail, but beware, there are some differences!

DIRECTIONS: Leave the car park by the road and walk back down 70m as far as the signpost to 'Great Orme Mines, Ski Centre, and Llandudno'.

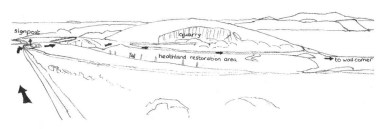

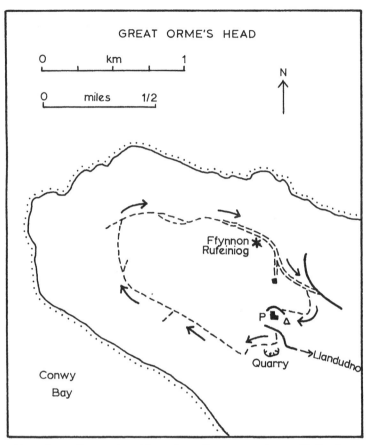

GREAT ORME'S HEAD

Ffynnon
Rufeiniog

P

Quarry

→Llandudno

Conwy
Bay

Here, leave the road and turn down the grassy slope with the fence on your right. At the end of the fence, bear right to keep the main gorse and heather patch to your right.

This patch of heather is in a heathland restoration area. The soil is thin on this steep slope and vulnerable to natural erosion. Also, years of trampling have taken their toll on the vegetation. By limiting walkers to a few paths, it is hoped that the vegetation will recover.

At the bottom, turn right to walk between the quarry and the heather with an intermittent fence on your right. Continue in the general direction of Puffin Island, off Anglesey, in the distance until you reach the wall corner and the nature trail post. Here, keep the wall to your right.

CONWY ESTUARY

Ahead lies Anglesey, separated from the mainland by the Menai Straits, with Puffin Island as the most easterly tip of Anglesey. The Carneddau Mountains lie above Penmaenmawr. The view to the south opens up as you walk by the wall revealing the estuary of the Conwy where the river flows into the Irish Sea.

600m along the wall, ignore the two posts with arrows to the left, but continue straight on.

These posts mark the Monks Path. This route was used over 500 years ago by monks who lived at the Abbey on Llandudno's West Shore. The building is now ruined.

As the wall swings right, the landscape ahead opens up to reveal a change from smooth grass to rougher grass, gorse and limestone 'pavement'. At the bottom of the first slope, take the wider path between gorse rather than the narrow path adjacent to the wall, as the latter becomes rather bumpy. Continue between the gorse, veering slightly away from the wall.

The patches of rocky 'pavement' reveal the underlying limestone. During the ice age over 10,000 years ago, this area was covered by a great ice sheet from the Irish Sea, which scraped away the surface soil and rock. Although vegetation has slowly covered parts of the rock, some still remains bare. The flat areas of rock are referred to as clints while the gullies, which have been weathered by rain water and freeze-thaw, are called grykes.

The path narrows and winds between rocky 'pavements', but heads in the general direction of the limestone rock which looks like a triangulation pillar on the skyline. Join a broader grassy path crossing diagonally from the parking area to the left behind you. Bear right along this path and pass between the wall corner on your right and the nature trail post on your left. Take the left fork between the gorse rather than the right fork adjacent to the wall.

Between here and where you rejoin the wall, there are scattered rocks on the left. Most of these are pedestals of more resistant rock which have not been weathered as much as the surrounding area. The rock adjacent to post 7 is nicknamed The Free Trade Rock as it is claimed deals were struck here in the past.

Drop down the hill to the wall corner, and then continue with the wall on your right as the grassy path becomes a stony track uphill.

At post 8 is Ffynnon Rufeiniog which translates as Roman Well. However, carbon dating has revealed that spoil from small copper mines nearby are from about 3500 B.C. This puts them into the Bronze Age, the same era as the main Orme mine. The well would have been the water supply for separating the ore from the rock. There are a few other wells on the Orme but elsewhere the water is scarce due to the limestone rock.

Pass the gate and ignore the farm drive on your right.

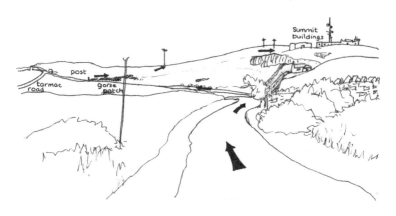

Many paths lead back to the summit but most are steep. These directions take you up the most gentle route. 70m before joining the tarmac road, turn right at the nature trail post up a grassy path. Follow the nature trail posts, gradually bearing right to the summit. It is worth pausing to look at the views across to the Little Orme behind you. Join the tarmac road which curves around the summit buildings to return to the car park.

16 Llyn Llydaw on Snowdon

This is a walk into the Snowdon Massif with surprisingly little effort. The route, on the famous Miners' Track, involves a gentle climb to the lake in a spectacular corrie with the summit of Snowdon as a backdrop. The surface is good for the majority of the way and enables you to feel that you are genuinely in a mountainous area.

Distance:	**4 miles / 6 km**
Total ascent:	**80m**
Surface:	**Gravel track with a few short rocky sections**
No. of stiles:	**0**
No. of kissing gates:	**0**
Need to pull or carry:	**Pull across four x 20m stretches**

HOW TO GET THERE: Take the A4086 between Capel Curig and Llanberis to the car park at Pen-y-Pass opposite the youth hostel. The charge is variable (£2/£4) depending on season and the car park is often full in peak season. However Sherpa buses run frequently from nearby villages during such times.

DIRECTIONS: At the far end of the lower car park, take the Miners' Track, a wide path which gently rises through the gate. It has a fine gravel surface. After $^1/_2$ mile (1 km), as the track rounds a corner, it becomes level.

Views of Snowdon summit, Yr Wyddfa, first appear, shortly followed by Llyn Teyrn below on your left. The track was built up at this point to carry small trucks to carry out the copper ore from the mines higher up. The row of old buildings near the lake is the ruin of some miners' barracks. The miners lived here from Monday morning to Saturday lunchtime, returning home for Sunday only. Life expectancy for the men in these barracks was only 40 years. Not surprisingly, the barracks were damp and were not inhabited for long.

As the path sweeps round behind Llyn Teyrn and starts to rise, between here and Llyn Llydaw, there are four rough patches where it may be necessary to pull the pushchair. However, none is longer than 20m. As you rise, the path converges with a pipeline.

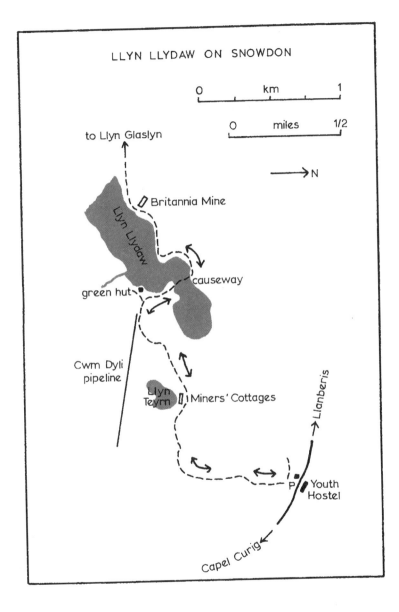

LLYN LLYDAW ON SNOWDON

to Llyn Glaslyn

Britannia Mine

Llyn Llydaw

causeway

green hut

Cwm Dyli
pipeline

Llyn
Teyrn

Miners' Cottages

Llanberis

P
Youth
Hostel

Capel Curig

O   km   1

O   miles   1/2

N

*This pipe was built in 1905 to power the hydro-electricity power
station at Cwm Dyli in Nant Gwynant below. It extracts water
from Llyn Llydaw and was originally intended to power a railway
line down to Beddgelert in one direction and Capel Curig and
Betws-y-Coed in the opposite direction. The railway was never
constructed but the power station continues to provide electricity
to the national grid. In the 1990's the pipeline was rebuilt
controversially on the surface as conservationists wanted it
below ground.*

Ignore the left fork leading towards the green hut at the top of the
pipeline; this is the start of the path up to Lliwedd, the peak to your left.
Continue to Llyn Llydaw, passing, on your left, a small beach with Yr
Wyddfa towering above.

*The effects of the Ice Age are all around you. The lake has
formed in a great corrie, scoured out by ice over 10,000 years
ago, while the mountains have been steepened and shattered
by frost action. To your left are rounded rocks, smoothed by
stones frozen into the base of the glacier. The hummocky
ground beyond the small pond is made of glacial deposits.
This dramatic landscape has many stories associated with it.
There is a legend that it was on the slopes to the left of Yr
Wyddfa that King Arthur finally met his death in a battle with the
Saxons. The dying king was carried down to Llyn Llydaw and
borne away across the lake on a black barge containing three
beautiful women!*

The path passes through a small cutting and then crosses Llyn
Llydaw on a causeway.

*The causeway was built in 1853 by miners. Prior to that, all the
copper ore was transported across the lake on a raft which
ferried the horses and carts. On two occasions the boat sank.*

From here, follow the path around the lake side, where it is possible to
get the pushchair to just beyond the mine buildings on your right,
although there is one 60m rough stretch.

*During the 18th and 19th centuries, there were numerous
copper mines on Snowdon of which this one, Britannia Mine,
was the most famous. The ore was brought down by aerial
ropeway from Llyn Glaslyn, where it was mined, to these*

buildings which are the remains of the mill. As well as copper, other ores were also mined, including manganese for steel-making, ochre for paint and calamine for medicinal purposes. The red colouring of the rocks by the minerals gives the name to the mountain above – Crib Goch or Red Ridge. In 1907 the track was passable by motor car up to this point.

BRITANNIA MINE

Once round the bend beyond the mine buildings, the path starts to rise quite steeply towards Llyn Glaslyn, another 160m above. It becomes rougher and here it is necessary to turn round and retrace your steps to the car park.

Yr Wyddfa gets its name from the word 'Gwyddfa' meaning grave or tomb. The legend is told that the giant, Rhita Gawr, was buried on the summit after being killed by King Arthur. Rhita Gawr was renowned for wearing a cloak made from the beards of all the kings he had slain.

Once back it is worth walking through the upper car park to a spectacular view. Follow the tarmac track for 60m to a narrow gap in the wall. This is the start of the Pyg Track, another famous path leading to Yr Wyddfa. At the base of the steps there are fine views down the Llanberis Pass.

17 A Walk Around Moel Trefriw

It is a circular walk on the hills to the east of the Conwy Valley overlooking Llanrwst and the mountains of Snowdonia. This is a strenuous walk but the views make the effort worthwhile. Parts of the route can be muddy and it also involves a 500m pull up a steep, rough track.

Distance:	**3¹/₂ miles / 5.5 km**
Total ascent:	**230m**
Surface:	**Rough tracks, sometimes muddy, and tarmac roads**
No. of stiles:	**0**
No. of kissing gates:	**0**
Need to pull or carry:	**Pull on several rough stretches including one uphill**

HOW TO GET THERE: From Betws-y-Coed, take the A470 towards Llanrwst. After less than ¹/₂ mile, turn right up the steep, single track road, signposted to Capel Garmon. At the T-junction, turn left and park anywhere on the left where the road is wide enough.

DIRECTIONS: Continue along the road to Bod Hyfryd on your right. Turn right up the tarmac road to the left of Bod Hyfryd. The road rises, and then dips steeply before rising again to a gate. Go through the gate and, just before the farmhouse of Gwninger, turn sharp right up an old

AT GWNINGER

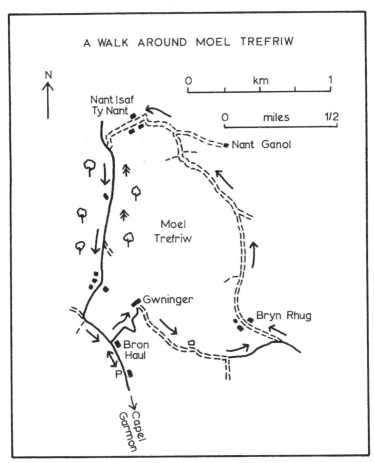

A WALK AROUND MOEL TREFRIW

road which has been tarmaced in the past.

The surface deteriorates as you rise and it is necessary to pull the pushchair for the next 600m until the track flattens out and the surface improves. When you stop for rests you are rewarded by views across the Conwy Valley, Gwydir Forest and the mountains beyond. At the gate adjacent to the ruin of Ffridd, go straight ahead along the lane. The surface improves and it is usually possible to push here although there are occasional muddy stretches after farm vehicles have been working. At the second gate, ignore the track joining from the right and continue to the next junction.

Turn sharp left through the gateway to Bryn Rhug and follow the farm drive to enter the farmyard by the gate. Leave the main buildings to your left and continue straight ahead (all the dogs are chained). Go through the gate at the far end of the farmyard and follow the track (which can be muddy) to the next gate; it is probably necessary to pull most of the 300m.

Once through the second gate, the surface gradually improves and becomes tarmac as it descends around Moel Trefriw, the hill to your left. After a mile, bear left where the Nant Ganol farm track joins from the right. Turn sharp left through Ty Nant farmyard with Ty Nant and Nant Isaf on your left. Continue down to the road and cross the cattle grid. **! The wheels easily become stuck between the bars.** Turn left up the hill back to your car. **! Look out for traffic.**

18 Llanddwyn Island and Newborough Warren

This walk in south west Anglesey meanders through pine forests before crossing the sandy Newborough beach, which can be hard going if the sand is a soft. The island of Llanddwyn can be reached on all but the highest of tides and there follows an undulating path of gravel and shells which allows you to explore most parts of this remote and historic island. There are sandy beaches, a lighthouse and, in the summer, a small exhibition. It is also a nature reserve. Although it is a fairly flat walk, it is quite strenuous due to the nature of the surface, but your efforts are rewarded with wonderful views.

Distance:	**3¹/₂ miles / 6 km**
Total ascent:	**50m**
Surface:	**Stony track, rocky / muddy / sandy / gravel paths (soft in places)**
No. of stiles:	**0**
No. of kissing gates:	**0**
Need to pull or carry:	**Max. 600m pull along beach, short stretches on Llanddwyn**

For map, see page 74

HOW TO GET THERE: Take the A5 across the Britannia Bridge to Anglesey. Immediately over the bridge, turn left, and left again along the A4080 to follow the signs to Newborough. Once in the village, turn left down the road beside the White Lion public house, signposted to the beach/traeth. There follows a 1 mile drive through pine plantations to the car park. There is a £2 charge at an automatic barrier for which the correct amount of coins are needed.

DIRECTIONS: Return to the small 'roundabout' at the car park entrance and take the road with a yellow and black barrier, to the right of the toilets. A path leads round the side of the barrier and the route then continues on a track parallel to the coast for over ¹/₂ mile (1 kilometre), at first on tarmac. It soon becomes stony; however, it is easy to push the pushchair

Most of the sand dunes at Newborough Warren are covered with Corsican Pines which help to stabilize the shifting sands. Marram grass has been planted here since Elizabethan times, giving rise to an industry making ropes, mats and baskets which died out only at the beginning of 20th century.

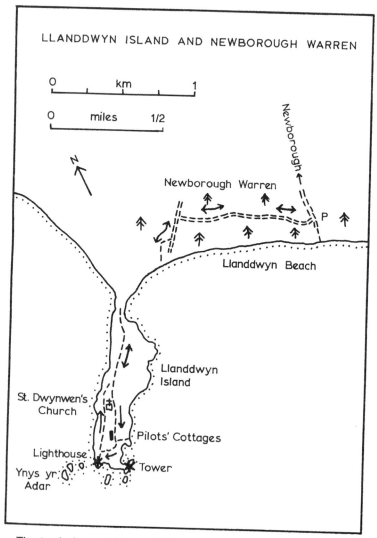

LLANDDWYN ISLAND AND NEWBOROUGH WARREN

Newborough

Newborough Warren

Llanddwyn Beach

P

Llanddwyn Island

St. Dwynwen's Church

Pilots' Cottages

Lighthouse

Ynys yr Adar

Tower

The track rises slightly, and then as it starts to drop downhill, there appear the first views of the sea and Llanddwyn Island through the recently thinned trees. After another 330m, at a T-junction, turn left towards the sea. At a small parking area, almost on the beach, turn right past the sign 'No parking or driving on the beach'. The way narrows to a sandy track between dunes where it is necessary to pull the pushchair for 30m before the path becomes stony again. It stops abruptly at the beach where the end of the track has been washed away in a winter gale. There is now a short scramble or slide down to the beach for which it may be necessary to carry the pushchair.

Turn right along the beach for 250m to the sandy causeway at Llanddwyn Island. It can be hard work pulling the pushchair along the beach as the surface is variable, but the hardest sand is usually to be found nearest the sea. Cross the causeway to the noticeboard. N.B. This area is covered at the highest tides for a short period.

Llanddwyn Island is a Nature Reserve managed by the Countryside Commission for Wales. It has this status because of its wildlife, particularly seabirds and coastal plants. Llanddwyn is also renowned for its historic sites associated with early Christian settlers.

Take the main path to the right of the noticeboard, surfaced with crushed shells. At the time of print they are rather soft and it is necessary to pull the pushchair but they should settle and become firmer over time. At the top of the hill take the left fork which is the main path and also has the better surface. Here you have the first views of the lighthouse.

On the right is an enclosure for sheep. These are Soay sheep, believed to be the oldest breed in the world, and were kept as long ago as Neolithic times.

Continue along the path passing the Celtic cross on your left and the abbey ruins on your right.

These are the remains of the 16th century church which was built on the site of a much older church. It was dedicated to St. Dwynwen, a saint who settled here in the 5th century. She is known as the Welsh St. Valentine as it was claimed that movements of a sacred fish or eel in her holy well (sited just beyond the cleft in the rock on the skyline to the right of the ruins) could foretell the fortunes of lovers. The legend is that she asked to be taken up there as she was dying in order to see her last sunset.

LLANDDWYN ISLAND

Another 200m along the path brings you to the Pilots' Cottages and Pilots' Cove.

The cottages were built to house the four pilots who were responsible for manning the lighthouse and piloting vessels into Caernarfon Harbour. Two cottages house an exhibition and are open to the public in the summer months. The older lighthouse was built in 1800 in the style of a windmill while the newer one replaced it in 1845. The new lighthouse is no longer in service but the older tower now houses an automatic light. The cannon was sited originally nearer Newborough village and was used to alert the crew of the lifeboat. Pilots' Cove is a lovely sandy beach and is usually sheltered from the wind by the wall.

Take the path to the right, directly beyond the last cottage, and continue straight on where a path joins from the left. Turn left up the steps to the lighthouse. They are negotiable with a pushchair, but bumpy.

The views from the lighthouse across to the mainland are, from the left, Snowdonia, including Snowdon summit directly above the old lighthouse, the Llyn, including the three peaks of Yr Eifl, and the coastline extending west towards Bardsey Island. The isolated rock is Ynys yr Adar (Bird Island). To the north is Rhoscolyn Beacon, with Holyhead Mountain beyond and the expanse of sands of Malltraeth Bay in the foreground.

Return to the path junction at the bottom of the steps. You can return across the island by the same route, or, for the more intrepid, there is a scenic detour.

Detour: Take the steep path up to the left by the cross. The surface of the path varies between broken shell, hard mud, grass, and rough paving and, although it is narrow in places, it is pushable for most of the way. At the top of the hill there are fantastic views across the whole island and into the coves on the northwest side. Continue to follow the yellow posts as the path rises over a knoll, then drops down to rejoin the outward path. Turn left.

Retrace your steps to the car park.

19 A Walk Around Llyn Elsi

Llyn Elsi lies in the Gwydir Forest above Betws-y-Coed. The walk involves, at the start, a strenuous climb of 220m (height) on stony tracks, with the whole of the first $^1/_2$ mile (1 km) being steep as well. However your effort is rewarded by spectacular views over the Snowdonia Mountains and a beautiful undulating walk around the shores of the lake on a gravel path. There are plenty of places to picnic near the lake.

Distance:	**4 miles / 7 km**
Total ascent:	**250m**
Surface:	**Stony tracks and gravel paths**
No. of stiles:	**0**
No. of kissing gates:	**0**
Need to pull or carry:	**Pull up 800m on first hill and few short steep stretches around lake. Also 21 steps up.**

HOW TO GET THERE: Take the A5 to Betws-y-Coed and park in the village. There are plenty of car parks but limited roadside parking.

DIRECTIONS: Leave the A5 by turning up either of the two roads adjacent to St. Mary's Church. At the top behind the church, take the forest track to the right of the stone bungalow, signposted to Llyn Elsi. Beyond the barrier there follows an 800m long stiff climb, up which it is easier to pull a pushchair. At a stream the path veers right and for a short stretch is slightly rockier. Ignore the path turning right over the bridge by a bench and continue upwards.

After a further 100m, a grassy path leads off to the left rising gently to a viewpoint. It is worth the detour of 100m to a bench although it is not possible to take a pushchair the last 50m.

> *There are views northwards down the Conwy Valley towards Llanrwst. There is a clearly contrasting land use between the two valley sides due to the geology. The steep west slope of resistant slates and volcanic rocks is covered in conifers, while on the east slope the softer shale allows pastoral farming.*

On return to the main track the route now rises much more gently all the way to the lake. There are several track junctions between here and

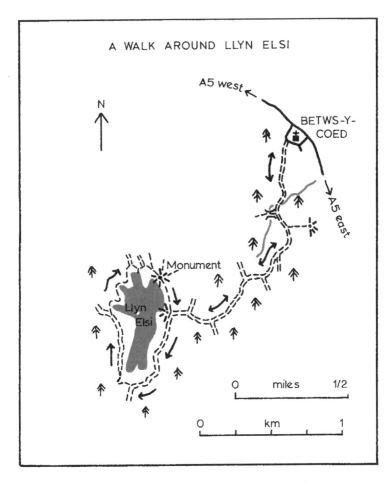

A WALK AROUND LLYN ELSI

Llyn Elsi. Ignoring all footpaths, the directions are as follows:

1. Straight on where the grassy track forks left.
2. 200m later, turn right.
3. After a further 150m, bear left.
4. After another 400m continue straight on, ignoring the track on your left.
5. After a further 140m, at the T-junction, turn left.

   ! Beware of mountain bikes as the route has now converged with a cycle way. As this track drops gently down to the lake, the view gradually opens up in front of you.

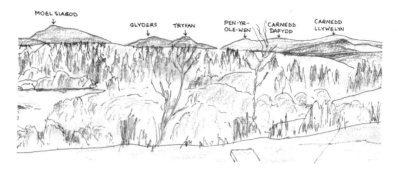

The mountain dominating the skyline is Moel Siabod, with the Glyders and the three peaked Tryfan to their right. The mountain range to your right is the Carneddau, a long high ridge extending almost to the north coast.

At the lake, the track swings left and follows the lake on your right. At the far end, the track sweeps right to parallel the dam at the southern end. It then winds slightly downhill. Where it starts to rise again on a sharp left bend, take the gravel path which rises very steeply between rocky outcrops. This path is excessively steep and it is necessary to pull the pushchair, but fortunately it flattens immediately around the bend. The gravel path winds across a felled area, bearing right over two drainage ditches and undulating between rocky outcrops, before it joins a track end. Continue straight ahead along the track.

At the highest point, views of the lake reappear. Carry on for a further 100m until you see an inlet of the lake below with a path on the far side.

! Turn right carefully down the ridiculously steep gravel path, bearing right at the bottom to cross the inlet by a bridge. The next section to the dam is along a pleasant undulating path mostly at the water's edge through birch woodland and around promontories. Some of the undulations are short but steep and it may be necessary to pull in places. There is also a wooden walkway across a boggy area.

As you approach the dam, turn left up a flight of steps, then wind down again to the far side of the dam. Cross the bridge and continue straight ahead, ignoring two paths on your left and one on your right.

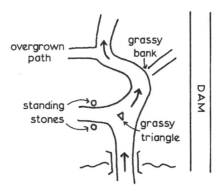

There is a short uphill followed by a flat section. Ignore the muddy path which joins on the left and continue up another longer hill to the monument. The gravel is beginning to become washed away in places leaving a rutted surface so it may be necessary to pull.

The monument records the gift of the lake to the people of Betws-y-Coed by the Earl of Ancaster in 1914. The Ancaster Estate at that time owned most of the land in the area and even today is a major land owner. Llyn Elsi still provides water for the people of Betws-y-Coed. Prior to the formation of this reservoir, there were several smaller lakes on the site.

Keep to the right of the monument and take the gravel path almost straight ahead down towards the lake. **! It is very steep**. At the bottom it undulates along the lake side, with some steep drops, until it rejoins the track of your outward journey. Turn left to retrace your steps to the village. To remind you of the route, below are listed the directions to take at each track junction:

1. Turn right.
2. Straight on.
3. Turn right.
4. Turn left.
5. Straight on down to the road.

20 Lôn Las Ogwen: Bethesda to the Sea

Lôn Las Ogwen is one of the cycle and walking routes which have been created by Gwynedd County Council on old railway lines. This walk starts in Bethesda on rural footpaths through woods and open countryside which can be quite hard going, but the second half is easy as it joins the old railway ending at the former slate dock at Bangor. It is a one way walk but it is most convenient to leave your car in Bangor at the end of the walk and catch the bus to Bethesda (or Tregarth for the second easier half). There are plans to extend the Lôn Las Ogwen from Bethesda to Tregarth which would make an easy alternative to the start of this walk. No date has been confirmed at the time of going to print.

Distance:	**6 miles / 9 km (4 miles / 6 km from Tregarth)**
Total ascent:	**60m (0m from Tregarth)**
Surface:	**Slate and grassy paths (Gravel path from Tregarth)**
No. of stiles:	**0**
No. of kissing gates:	**10 but 2 negotiable (0 from Tregarth)**
Need to pull or carry:	**300-400m pull depending on conditions, lift over kissing gates (None from Tregarth)**

For map of Bethesda to Tregarth, see page 84

HOW TO GET THERE: From the A55, take the A5122 to Bangor. On the outskirts of Bangor, at the 30mph sign, turn right signposted to Porth Penrhyn. Fork left to enter Porth Penrhyn and cross the bridge with white railings. As the road swings left, park almost straight ahead to the left of a white building 'Old Port Office-Hen Swyddfa'r Porthladd'. An arrow to the right indicates the end of your walk.

Retrace your steps to the main road and turn left for 100m to the bus stop. Nos.6, 7 or 66 take you to Bethesda or nos. 6 or 7 to Tregarth. Telephone Arriva Buses on 01492 592111 for details.

DIRECTIONS: From Tregarth: With your back to the village shop, turn right along the main road past the Shiloh Chapel for 200m to the start of the Lôn Las Ogwen cycle track. Follow the directions from the # on page 86.

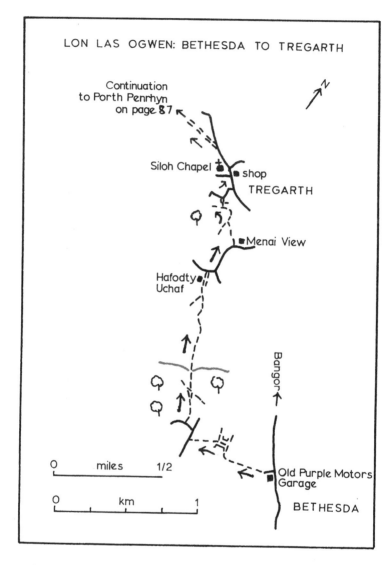

LON LAS OGWEN: BETHESDA TO TREGARTH

Continuation to Porth Penrhyn on page 87

Siloh Chapel

shop

TREGARTH

Menai View

Hafodty Uchaf

Bangor

miles 1/2

km 1

Old Purple Motors Garage

BETHESDA

DIRECTIONS: From Bethesda: Walk down the main road in the direction of Bangor to Station Road, adjacent to the Londis shop. Turn down Station Road and, at the end, pass through the wide kissing gate signposted to '4 Valleys Path'. This wide path next to the river soon leaves the industry behind. Turn left over the footbridge across the Afon Ogwen and continue straight up the slate path. There is a short steep stretch up which it is necessary to pull. It levels out and joins the road at a kissing gate through which you might just squeeze the pushchair. Turn right. **! There is no pavement,** but after 50m take the road left uphill, signposted to 'Mynydd Llandygai'. Immediately after the 30mph sign, take the gravel path to the right with a footpath sign. In places there are slate slabs and it is flanked by a slate fence, traditional of this area.

Enter the broadleafed woodland via a narrow kissing gate. Most of the woodland path is pushable although some sections may be too hard going after rain or when the path is overgrown. The path dips at first, but, as it starts to rise up the hill, take the right fork along the narrower path. After 25m at another junction of paths, go straight on to the right of a red topped post. Cross a small stream and leave the woods by another narrow kissing gate.

Go straight ahead across the field, keeping the field boundary to your right. Lift the pushchair over the narrow kissing gate, and cross straight over the track, heading up the arrowed path through the gorse. It will be necessary to pull for much of the next 300m. Keep the wall on your left to the top where the view opens up at a gap in the wall.

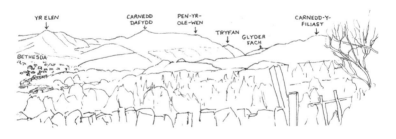

The path continues with the wall on your right but soon veers away from it. There are several different routes to take but all ultimately rejoin.

As the paths close with the wall, pass through the gap. Continue straight on across the next field of bracken towards the rocky outcrop. The path passes to the left of the outcrop and enters a thicket. On re-emerging at the far side, it continues ahead to rejoin the wall again at a kissing gate. Lift the pushchair over the gate, and then cross two more fields on a clear path. Leave the second field by the kissing gate or the field gate and walk down the track to the road, with Hafodty Uchaf on your left.

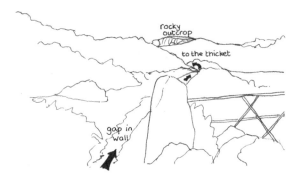

Turn right along the road, and then bear left at the junction. As the road sweeps right, turn left along the drive of Menai View at the footpath sign. Pass through the wide kissing gate and walk along the muddy path. Ignore the kissing gate in the chain link fence on your right, and continue through the next kissing gate ahead. It is narrow but there is an adjacent field gate. After passing under the wires, bear right at the T-junction in paths. Lift the pushchair over the next kissing gate to follow the path as it sweeps left around the woodland boundary wall. Immediately before the next gate across the path, turn right down 11 steps and continue straight ahead down the hill past the house to a small lane. Here, wind downhill to the B-road in Tregarth. There is a village shop and a pub which serves very limited food.

Turn left along the pavement to follow the B-road past the Shiloh Chapel for 300m to the signed start of Lôn Las Ogwen.

> *The Penrhyn Slate Quarry suffered numerous strikes and lock outs at the end of 19th century. During the 3 year strike, many of the blacklegs lived in Tregarth rather than Bethesda for their own safety. It is claimed that, during a service at the Siloh Chapel, when two blacklegs walked in, the entire congregation walked out.*

\# From now on the route is easy with a fine gravel surface and wide gateways.

> *Two old railway lines follow similar routes down as far as the main line near Bangor. One was the passenger branch line from Bangor to Bethesda. The other was the narrow gauge railway which was built by the Penrhyn Estate to carry slate from the Penrhyn Quarries at Bethesda to Porth Penrhyn where you left*

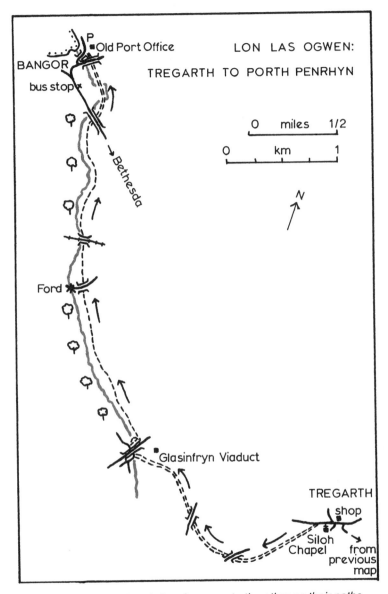

LON LAS OGWEN:

TREGARTH TO PORTH PENRHYN

your car. The walk switches from one to the other as their paths cross, but here starts on the passenger line.

After the second bridge, the path is joined by Afon Cegin which follows the path for most of the way. Drop down to cross the B4366. **! This is a busy road.** Follow the gravel path along an embankment.

The embankment widens as it carried both railway lines. The left hand line (the narrow gauge railway) starts to drop away and just before the Glasinfryn Viaduct, it crosses underneath your route at a narrow bridge. From there it parallels the passenger line on the right hand side passing the near side of the farm.

At the end of the viaduct the path bears left to join a road. Turn right under the A55, and then right again to join Lôn Bach. Ignore the left fork, but stay on the level path which parallels the A55 for 100m. Bear left through a gateway to join the old quarry railwayline. This is a pleasant stretch through woodland, with numerous paths down to the stream.

FORD NEAR LLANDEGAI

As you approach the next bridge, the gates on your left lead on to a road. Here you can see a ford with the old metal footbridge next to it. Up the hill you can also see the railway bridge of the Bethesda line as it veers away towards Bangor to join the main line.

Continue along the old railway under the bridge and then shortly pass under the viaduct which carries the main London to Holyhead line.

There is evidence of the old and new industry alongside each other. There are remnants of the old slate fence from the quarry days, while beyond are the new buildings of the Llandygai Industrial Estate.

Pass under one more bridge, and over two as the Afon Cegin meanders under the path.

Lôn Bach railway was built between 1870 and 1879. Before that, slate was taken by packhorse along the old road built in 1801. Pont Marchogion, the 18th century bridge on your left, was part of the old road. The quarry line closed in 1962 as slate declined, but also as roads regained their importance once again.

Pass under the last bridge to return to your car.

21 Moel Famau and the Jubilee Tower

Although not in the Snowdonia Range, Moel Famau is a 'proper' mountain at 554m height. It lies in the Clwydian Range, east of Ruthin, and part of the walk follows the Offa's Dyke long distance footpath. The last 500m are steep uphill and a bit rough, but the views and the sense of achievement make the effort worthwhile. There is the option of returning via the forest to make a circular walk. There are toilets and picnic benches 1 mile further along the road from the car park.

Distance:	**3 miles / 5 km** **(4 miles / 6 km for forest return)**
Total ascent:	**244m** **(300m for forest return)**
Surface:	**Stony paths and tracks**
No. of stiles:	**0** **(1 for forest return)**
No. of kissing gates:	**0**
Need to pull or carry:	**500m pull up last hill**

HOW TO GET THERE: From Ruthin, take the A494 towards Mold. At Llanbedr Dyffryn Clwyd (1¹/₂ miles), take the very narrow road, Lôn Cae Glas, to the left **after** the church. It is signed 'unsuitable for heavy goods vehicles'. Immediately before the third cattle grid, turn **left** into the pay and display car park.

DIRECTIONS: From the car park take the signed path to the right of the information board about Moel Famau. It rises gently on fine gravel, curving round the side of the hill. Keep to the main wide path, ignoring all paths to the left and right.

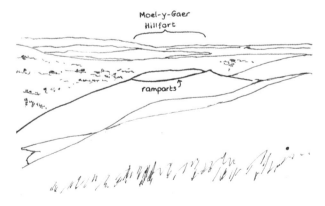

Moel-y-Gaer
Hillfort

ramparts

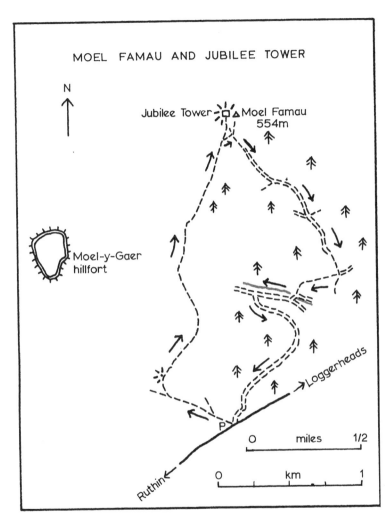

MOEL FAMAU AND JUBILEE TOWER

Moel-y-Gaer was occupied from 500 B.C. to 43 A.D., immediately prior to the Roman Conquest. The remains of the double ramparts can be seen clearly, and these were reinforced on the east side where natural defences were weakest. Moel-y-Gaer is one of three hillforts built to defend the mountains from attackers in the Vale of Clwyd below.

After the bench on your left there is a rougher section as far as the top of the next rise across which it may be necessary to pull. Once over the brow of the hill, the path improves again and you have your first glimpse of the summit ahead. There follows a section which is virtually flat across the heather moorland.

The path follows the route of the Offa's Dyke long distance footpath although at this point the path does not actually follow the original earthworks. The purpose of Offa's Dyke is not certain, but is believed to have been constructed by King Offa in the 8th century to mark the western limits of his kingdom. There is evidence of the management along this part of the path to control erosion.

At the end of the trees on your right, the path starts its final ascent to Jubilee Tower. It is necessary to pull from here most of the way to the summit.

JUBILEE TOWER

The summit is dominated by the remains of the Jubilee Tower although the natural highest point is at the triangulation pillar to your right. The tower was built in 1810 to commemorate the Golden Jubilee of King George III, but it was destroyed sixteen years later by a storm. In the centre of the ruins is a labelled sketch of the view in all four directions. On a clear day places as far as Cader Idris and Runcorn Bridge can be seen.

Return by the same route or take the forest return.

Forest return: Retrace your steps down the same path for 65m to the first left fork signed with a blue footprint. Cross the stile adjacent to the gate.

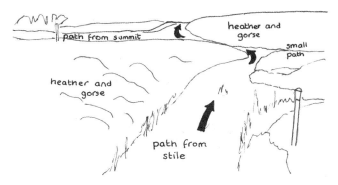

After 50m, at a staggered crossroads among heather, fork left and then immediately right onto a wider stony path. This path is overly steep downhill at first, but, as it sweeps left, it flattens out and widens to a track. As it enters a coniferous plantation, ignore the path to your right and a second track joining on the right later.

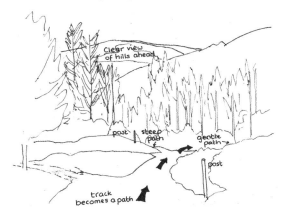

The track deteriorates to a path and reaches crossroads. Turn right along the path through larches to the next track. Bear right, and right again along the main track. At the end of the long straight section, with a stream on your right, turn left along the main track, fortunately before the path ahead starts to rise steeply. The track rises steadily as it curves around the hillside before the views reappear at the brow of the hill. It drops down gently to the barrier at the road. Turn right through the gate adjacent to the cattle grid and turn right again into the car park.

22 A Walk Around Llyn Brenig

Llyn Brenig is a large reservoir on the Denbigh Moors and around it is a circular walk along a mixture of tracks, paths and road. Most of the walk is easy going but on the northern end of the lake where the footpath is rougher, there is a road alternative. There is a visitor centre at the start with a café (open weekends only in the winter).

Distance:	**10 $1/2$ miles / 17 km**
Total ascent:	**110m**
Surface:	**Stony tracks, tarmac, some muddy paths (can be avoided)**
No. of stiles:	**0**
No. of kissing gates:	**0**
Need to carry or pull:	**Pull or carry on muddy stretches (can be avoided on road)**

For map, see page 96

HOW TO GET THERE: From Betws-y-Coed, take the A5 towards Llangollen. At Cerrigydrudion (12 miles), turn left and left again up the B4501 signed to Llyn Brenig. After another $3 1/2$ miles turn right down to the Visitor Centre and follow the signs to the car park. It is pay and display (£1). If the first gate is padlocked, park on the roadside. Walk down the right fork immediately before the gate and join the route at the beginning of the dam.

DIRECTIONS: From the car park, take the path over the bridge to the Visitor Centre. From the lower end of the Visitor Centre, turn right along the shoreline on a tarmac road. Where the road sweeps right uphill, go through the small wooden gate to the left of the large gate, signed 'Lake Walk $10 1/2$ miles'. At the end of the footpath turn left along the track across the dam.

> *The dam was constructed in 1976 to create a reservoir to supply water to north east Wales. It is 45m deep and a farm was drowned in the creation of the reservoir.*

At the end of the dam, turn left along the lakeside track. It passes through two gates and at the second enters the forest. Here the track veers right away from the lake through trees. Current felling provides occasional views of the lake but this may also create new tracks. Ignore any track to your right and keep the lake about 100m away to your left.

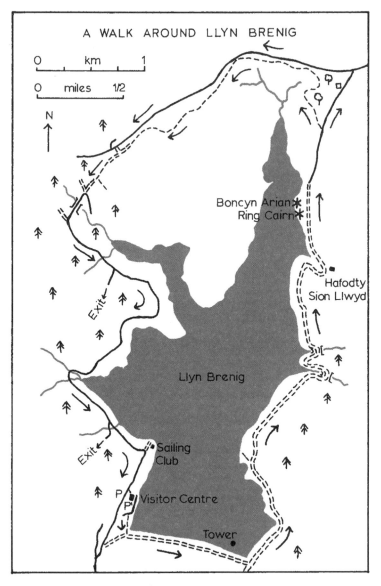

A WALK AROUND LLYN BRENIG

N

Boncyn Arian ✳
Ring Cairn ✳

Hafodty
Sion Llwyd

Exit

Llyn Brenig

Exit

Sailing
Club

P Visitor Centre
P

Tower

As the view opens up ahead, the track bears right and then turns sharp left to round the head of an inlet of the lake. The track immediately rounds a second smaller inlet and passes through a gate.

This part of the walk is across moorland. At an altitude of 380m, with high rainfall and peaty soils, only a limited range of plants can grow here. Areas of heather have been cut to encourage new shoots which provide food for grouse. The area is also grazed by sheep in the summer, but without them the moorland would slowly return to woodland which is its natural state. The whole 2 mile length of the lake can be seen from here.

HAFODTY SION LLWYD

After 800m of flat moorland, a third inlet is rounded. At its head lies Hafodty Sion Llwyd in its peaceful surroundings. At this point the route coincides with the Archaeological Trail and after a further 400m you pass the conspicuous Ring Cairn and burial mound of Boncyn Arian.

Boncyn Arian
burial mound

Llyn Brenig

4000 year old
Ring Cairn

Continue to the gate and car park (with toilets in summer). Keep to the right hand side of the car park and head up the tarmac road. At the top of the steep rise the signed footpath forks left. Here you have a choice of remaining on the road which adds a mile to the total length but avoids the rough muddy paths, or taking the rough path which involves some pulling.

Road: Continue up the road to the T-junction. Turn left along the B4501 for $1^1/_2$ miles (2.5 km). Although the traffic travels fast, there is little of it and it is a wide open road. At the top of the long hill, turn left along a track with a cycle route sign. At the T-junction turn right and follow the directions from the ** on page 99.

Footpath: The signed path which winds across moorland is mostly grassy and there are only some sections where you need to pull. However the first 200m are very boggy after rain, but if you can manage this, there is nothing worse ahead.

The path heads towards a fenced area of trees bearing first right and then left to follow the boundary of the wooded area. It then heads towards a clump of trees. As it closes with the road embankment, there are some awkward stretches over a culvert where the path narrows.

At the small clump of trees, you again have a choice. It is easy to join the road at this point to avoid a rough uphill which can be very muddy, or, for the very intrepid, continue on the signed footpath. If you choose the road, turn left along the road, uphill. At the top, turn left along a track with a cycle route sign. At the T-junction, turn right and follow the directions from the ** on page 99.

For the intrepid: Head to the left of the trees. The path bears left over a small stream, and then rises on grass. There follows a hill up through the heather with some erosion controls including wooden barriers and stone slabs. Despite these and the fact it is narrow, it is possible to pull all the way. As the slope flattens out, the erosion controls stop and it becomes muddy in a few places where it may be necessary to lift the pushchair. As you approach a small heather-clad hill ahead to your right, turn right at a post to keep the small hill on your left. The path is much eroded here. As the path nears the road, turn left up a clear stony path to the top of the hill. The path gradually becomes a track and is pushable again. At the top, as a track joins from the right, continue straight on.

** **For all routes:** The track gradually narrows to a path which is rutted in places.

Above the trees to your right on the skyline lie the ruins of the shooting lodge, Gwylfa Hiraethog. It was built by Lord Davenport in 1913, but the changes in lifestyles brought about by the First World War caused it to be abandoned. It is known locally as the Wooden Palace or the Haunted House. On a clear day the mountains of Moel Siabod, Tryfan, the Glyders and the Carneddau are all visible.

As the path descends alongside the road, it is joined by trees on your right. After passing through a gate, enter the forest along the track and ignore the footpath to the left.

At the junction, join the tarmac road and head down hill (straight ahead). Cross the bridge, believed to be mediaeval, and walk up the hill beyond. At the top of the hill, turn left. There follows a 2$^1/_2$ mile (4km) stretch winding around the lake. Keep to the main road and ignore two roads off to the right, both signed 'Exit Allan'. **! From here to the end there may be traffic, but it is one-way towards you.** At Llyn Brenig Sailing Club, turn right.

If you look down the road through the sailing club to the far side of the lake, you can see the road opposite. These two roads joined across the valley prior to the reservoir.

Continue along the road back to the start.